MW00626032

The Loveless Family

For Alba—

The Loveless Family

Getting Past Estrangement and Learning How to Love

Love,
J.P.Bloch

Jon P. Bloch

 PRAEGER

AN IMPRINT OF ABC-CLIO, LLC
Santa Barbara, California • Denver, Colorado • Oxford, England

Library of Congress Cataloging-in-Publication Data

Bloch, Jon P.
   The loveless family : getting past estrangement and learning how to love / Jon P. Bloch.
      p. cm.
   Includes bibliographical references and index.
   ISBN 978-0-313-39273-3 (hardcopy : alk. paper) — ISBN 978-0-313-39274-0 (ebook)   1. Families—Psychological aspects.   2. Parenting.   3. Dysfunctional families.   4. Adult children of dysfunctional families.   5. Love.   I. Title.
   HQ515.B56   2011
   155.9'24—dc22   2011015070

ISBN: 978-0-313-39273-3
EISBN: 978-0-313-39274-0

15   14   13   12   11   1   2   3   4   5

This book is also available on the World Wide Web as an eBook.
Visit www.abc-clio.com for details.

Praeger
An Imprint of ABC-CLIO, LLC

ABC-CLIO, LLC
130 Cremona Drive, P.O. Box 1911
Santa Barbara, California 93116-1911

This book is printed on acid-free paper ∞

Manufactured in the United States of America

Contents

Introduction

Some years ago, I happened upon a TV show in which a celebrity was interviewed in his home. As he gave the reporter a tour of the house, he said one of the most profound things I have ever heard: "Home is where we love."

I have no idea what the celebrity's home life was actually like, but what he said got me thinking. Statistics tell us that the U.S. home is all too often *not* a place where people love. About 3.5 million episodes of family violence are reported each year in the United States.[1] One in four women experience domestic violence.[2] An average of three women and one man are murdered each day by their spouse.[3] About 1.25 million children experience child abuse or neglect each year.[4] Upwards of 5 children a day die from child abuse.[5] Almost 70 percent of all sexually abused children suffer the abuse from a family member.[6] Anyone who has ever watched a TV crime show knows that immediate family members are the first suspects when someone is murdered.

Yet even in less extreme households, love all too often appears to be in short supply. Indeed, simply from talking to people from many walks of life over the years, I have reached the sad conclusion that the loveless family is all too common. A sibling or parent dies, and the surviving 25- or 60-year-old adult sheds not a tear and feels little or nothing. Or maybe the only sadness she feels is that she doesn't feel sad, even though she is *supposed* to. I know any number of perfectly reasonable people who are far more likely to cry if a beloved pet dies than if a family member does. Person A may, as an infant, have lost his father, while Person B's father is alive and well—yet both seem to have had the *same* father, in terms of the father's lack of emotional presence.

Stories from ancient times up to the present moment indicate that people identify with families that are less than loving. The oldest stories in the Bible—Adam and Eve, Cain and Abel—have a lot to do with the absence of love. Greek myths abound with parents or siblings who destroy the happiness of relatives. And even the gods on Olympus often hated each other, despite being blood relations. From Shakespeare to soap operas and everything in between, there are books, plays, films, and TV shows that essentially depict what happens when families lack love. If no one thought such stories spoke to their own lives, there would not be so many of these popular tales.

Still, "Home is where we love," seems like something that *should* be true much more often than it apparently is. When I first heard these words, I felt like my lifetime quest to understand my own family added up to zero beside this straightforward insight.

"Home is where we love." This was so removed from my actual experience that I could barely comprehend it. Yet as I thought about it, I saw my family history with a new clarity. The real problem wasn't the occasional misfortune. Nor was it the frequent losses of temper that could lead to violence or—in some ways worse—people screaming things that they later said they did not mean. Looking back, there were people who today might be described as being substance abusers, chronically depressed, or as suffering from a range of psychological disorders. Yet I no longer believe that any or all of these issues were the real problem. There are families that withstand such troubles and worse, and grow closer through hardship. In my family—and perhaps your family as well—the real problem was that people did not know how to love. This meant that for all intents and purposes there *was* no love. Perhaps some people tried to love, perhaps some people did not—I do not know what truths lay inside other people. But while disdain or indifference was expressed quite unambiguously, I pretty much had to look under a microscope to find love.

Love is not a cure-all. You can raise your child with all the love in the world and he may still turn out to be an addict, suicidal, mentally ill, a career criminal, a murderer, a rapist, a child molester, a spouse beater, unmotivated to succeed, unable to make money, unable to move out of the house, unable maintain a healthy, intimate relationship—or any number of other things you never had in mind when you took on the role of a parent. Tragically, perhaps your child died, or was murdered, kidnapped, or molested due to circumstances utterly beyond your control. The *last* thing I'd want you to think upon reading this book is that it's automatically your fault that someone in your family had a difficult or undesirable life because you did not love them. Love does not negate the possibility—or rather, inevitability—of having problems. And the life choices some people make seem incomprehensible, regardless of how they were raised. For that matter, sometimes people who grew up feeling unloved become successful, and even find love.

But this book is *not* about happily ever after. It is about feeling little or no connection to the people that supposedly you have the strongest connections to of all—your family. It is about taking a deep breath and facing the extremely painful fact that you never felt loved in your family. And, just as painful, that because you were unloved you feel little, if any, love for your family in return.

In a society that places considerable emphasis on family values, on putting the family first, and so on, this admission means violating an unwritten rule that family members should always love each other— even if they don't get along, even if they are homicidal or sexually abusive. "I love my daughter but I don't like her," you might say. And maybe it's true. But maybe you don't love her either; you just think you're supposed to say that you do. Or you might say, "Of course I love you, you're my daughter." But if that's the only reason for the love, is it really love, or just something you're expected to say? To say out loud, "My father hates me," or "I don't love my mother," is unlikely to win you admiration from the general public. In many people's minds, talking negatively about your family means you have a chip on your shoulder, you're immature, you're blaming your problems on other people, you're disloyal, you're selfish, or you're a bad person. But nonetheless, the essential truth you feel inside doesn't change: you grew up feeling unloved and perhaps you still feel the same way.

There is another, more general taboo that this book addresses, albeit often implicitly: that while the United States (for example) is a world leader in rates of homicide and incarceration,[7] at the same time, no one is supposed to dislike anyone else. One risks social ostracism if one goes so far as to state that one even *hates* another person, or maybe a number of people. I have known many people with extremely hostile personalities who, at the same time, insist that they do not dislike or hate anyone. Supposedly, only bad people hate. "Well, of course I don't hate him because he's my brother; I just haven't communicated with him in 50 years." I would submit that while there may be many complex emotions swirling around in this dynamic, one of them maybe, just maybe, is hatred.

Even when people are prejudiced against certain kinds of people they may insist that it isn't about hate. I have seen members of famous racist organizations state on TV that their organization is not about hatred. People who spread lies about homosexuality insist that they hate the sin, not the sinner. The very notion of hate crimes remains controversial, as if there is no such thing. To use an extreme example, some people deny that the Holocaust happened, because surely people could not do such unspeakable things to fellow humans. But it happened.

So this is a book for people who are willing to consider that yes, there are people they do not like or love, and who do not like or love them in return—specifically here, family members. It is also a book for people who have not felt that they have had *permission* to admit their animosity toward family members to find a safe haven for their true feelings.

However—and this is important—this is *not* a book that endorses committing acts of physical or other kinds of harm to others or to yourself. If your anger or hatred is getting out of control, please seek professional help at once.

The notion of the loveless family needs to be put into historical and social context. Human history reveals many practices that we would now consider child abuse, but which were considered acceptable in their time and place. In many parts of the world, people still die relatively young and are far too busy dealing with famine or illness to worry about ways of behaving that have become important in our own society. The very notion of having a self varies across history and culture—individuality is a fluid concept. But the point is that we *do* live in our own time and place. We increasingly expect to live long lives, and it increasingly is expected that we communicate well and get along with other people. We also increasingly seek to make our own choices in life—and to hope we chose well, since our social world has become so complicated. The success of our personal and professional lives depends on having certain behavioral, emotional, and mental skills that do not apply to other times and places. But they apply to *our* time and place, and it simply is more difficult to succeed in this challenging world we live in without a strong foundation of supportive love and caring.

Also, let us bear in mind that we are living in an era of profound transition. Recent decades have seen dramatic reconsiderations of long-held beliefs regarding race, ethnicity, gender, sexual orientation, and disabilities. With change—even change for the better—comes uncertainty. In a dual-income marriage, how should the couple determine household and child-rearing responsibilities? When two-partnered people have different ethnic backgrounds or religions, how do they teach their children about culture and religion? When a family is of an ethnic minority group, how much should native traditions be preserved versus teaching their children to assimilate into the dominant culture? If a single person doubts she will ever be in a committed relationship, should she adopt a child and/or give birth to one on her own? What is the best child-custody arrangement in cases of divorce? How much conflict is normal in a blended family—that is to say, a family in which there is remarriage and hence stepparents and stepsiblings living under one roof? These and many other questions do not come with simple, magic answers. Still, when people love and care about each other, they do their best to arrive at the best solutions they are capable of.

Maybe you think about your family almost constantly, or maybe you try to think about them as little as possible. But if you come from a loveless family, most of the memories you have are, at best, tepid. When you think about growing up in your family, a dryness or coldness may seem to fill your heart. Or maybe your heart seems to bleed with sorrow, frustration, or rage over the endless times you felt utterly disqualified, as if you weren't even there. Or maybe the family took its anger out on you, or set up impossible goals for you to achieve. But in any case, they did not make you feel like a warm-blooded human being entitled to appropriate love and attention.

Until recently, if anyone had told me that their parents never loved them, or even when one of my own family members mentioned that she sometimes felt that there had been no love in our own family, I would think to myself, "Oh grow up, of course you were loved." I thought it was very immature for, say, a 40-year-old adult to talk like this. Wasn't he old enough to realize that most people do their best? Couldn't she learn to forgive? To stop living in the past?

But suddenly I decided I owed these people an apology. Because I realized the obvious: I never felt loved, either. Doing their best—or even forgiveness—wasn't the point. Whether my family did their best or not, and whether or not I could appreciate the pressures my own family were under at the time, I did not believe my family loved me. Nor was the point to stop living in the past. Daily life responsibilities keep most of us living in the present most of the time and there's no crime in reflecting on the past. It's *your* life; you can think about it as much as you want.

I'd been complimented for having done as well as I have, considering how my life started out. Yet despite having achieved a number of personal goals, my life often seems as difficult and stressful as ever. I still struggle with compliments—they seem unreal or untrustworthy. Goal achievement did not do for me what I hoped it would do. And despite all the complex explanations I had pursued over the years for why I was the way I was, I realized that the main problem was much simpler. When there has never been much love in your life, it's extremely difficult to feel happy, safe, confident, or proud.

Some people are afraid to consider that their families did not love them. Even if they were beaten within an inch of their lives they need to believe that the beatings were done out of love. Then there are people who are convinced they were unloved, and so they spend 24/7 trying to impress others with their achievements and their agreeable—or maybe larger than life—personalities. Yet even when such efforts succeed on the surface, outsiders have no idea how empty the unloved person may still feel. If it turns out that he or she is suicidal from loneliness, others are shocked. He had so many friends. She was so easy to get along with. He was always so much fun to be around. She never complained about anything. And I would add that it does not matter if you are single or partnered. In fact, I know divorced people who recall that being married was the loneliest, most loveless time of their lives.

A couple of years later another revelation from the TV reached me. A reality series involved a family that showed one child in particular struggling with unhappiness. Like many people, I've wondered if reality shows actually are more scripted than the audience is led to believe. But scripted or spontaneous, the mother said something like, "A mother is only as happy as her unhappiest child."

This, too, just about knocked me over. Were there mothers—or for that matter, fathers—who treated their children's problems as more than just a nuisance? Who didn't make it clear that the best times in their lives were before their children were born? Were there parental figures who wanted their child to be happy more than they wanted that child to idolize them? Who didn't reject their child if he complicated their lives? Once again, I could scarcely comprehend it.

Then, as if that weren't enough, the mother actually *listened* to what her daughter had to say, and treated her words with the utmost respect. The mother did not tell her daughter she was wrong to feel the way she did, or that, as the mother, she of course knew everything. The mother's goal was not to feed her own ego, or treat her daughter as though she were her personal possession, but to help her child find happiness. Even if it *was* scripted, it was nice to see.

It must be wonderful to grow up with love in your home, to feel that when you walk in the door people are glad to see you, and you are entering the place where you feel the most loved. But from an early age, entering my own home was about entering the place where love died. Any elation I felt from being with friends or from just being by myself came to a dead halt as I entered the door. I was in the way; people felt better before I came back home. I occasionally was told I was loved, but it never rang true, and I always felt vaguely depressed to hear this and would robotically reply, "I love you, too."

When I was a child, *family* still meant the extended family of aunts, uncles, and cousins. Consequently, visiting with these other relatives happened often. Yet it was more of the same, a matter of driving from one unfeeling place to another. Sometimes the absence of love produced volatile tempers that frightened me—so much so that I am still learning how to express my own anger or even to question some of the things that were said. Other times, these visits made for a lethargic, despairing interlude of the smallest of small talk that no glimmer of humor dared to enter. The grown-ups also had a habit of reverting to the language of the old country from which my grandparents came. I'm sure there were things that the grown-ups didn't want the children to hear, but it never occurred to them that the children—who did not speak this language—might feel excluded, as if the really important things that were said did not include them. Not to mention that it's boring to sit there for hours when the discussion is in a language you don't understand.

In short, these visits made me want to crawl out of my skin. By the time I was old enough to cross the street by myself, I would go for long walks alone to escape the oppressive nothingness—or sometimes ugliness—though of course I did not have such fancy words for it at the time. And if anyone missed me, it was never mentioned—though I was occasionally taken to task for not being what my family called *sociable.* But in the final analysis, it all forms a singular whole in my mind. What warm feelings of acceptance I experienced came from school friends—and sometimes their parents—or from kind neighbors. By about the age of 10, I went to bed *earlier* than I had to, just to have time and space away from the others in my family.

Dysfunctional Families?

Over the past few decades, much has been said about the dysfunctional family. The word *dysfunctional* is used to describe how a family fails to provide a safe and nurturing environment. If you are comfortable referring to your family as dysfunctional—if it works for you—then that's great. But personally, I've never liked the word *dysfunctional*. I think it sounds clinical and cold, and that it diminishes the emotional reality of life. It is like saying, "Let's perform sexual intercourse," rather than saying, "Let's make love." If I explain to someone about my early life, he may cut me off and say, "You had a dysfunctional family," as if that's all there was to it. I think it turns complex lived experience into some predictable disease such as the chicken pox, and everything seems distant and abstract rather than real and raw.

Besides, in many ways my family *did* function. Babies got their diapers changed and dangerous household chemicals were kept out of reach. No one died an accidental death before reaching adulthood. Dinner was served on time, and there was a protein, a starch, and a vegetable. Dishes got washed, rugs got vacuumed, and bills got paid. All this and more took hard work.

Also, since no one is perfect, there is no such thing as a perfect family. As I write this, much of the world is dying of starvation or disease. Yet even by the affluent standards of our own society, my family would not rank at the bottom of the list. We were lower middle class, and like many such families, there was worry about not seeming poor. But there were no habitual wife beaters or hardcore junkies. Children were not locked in basements. Adolf Hitler was not a member of my family, nor was Charles Manson.

In fact, if I were to pick up the phone right now, it would be possible to have superficially pleasant conversations with a number of relatives—though some I'd have to catch in a good mood. And since there are intelligent people in my family, I might even get sound advice or hear a thought-provoking opinion on a current issue. No one is just any one thing, so people in my own loveless family may well be highly regarded by outsiders as kind, thoughtful, and yes, loving.

Not only that, but there are people who might say: "I *did* love you; I just didn't know how to show it." And it is perfectly true that love can be difficult to express. Perhaps the good intentions account for *something*. That is up to you to decide. But, speaking for myself: whatever people's intentions were, whatever obstacles they had to face—and I include myself in all this—when it comes right down to it my family was a loveless family. Put us all in the same room and love dies. The elation you feel from a communication in which love has been exchanged—whether face-to-face, on the phone, or through the Internet—does not occur when I speak with my family, and I am reasonably certain that others in my family feel the same way. I say this without melodrama, as I know I am hardly alone in having a loveless family. And though I freely admit to harboring hurt and anger from the past, I do not seek to be malicious. For I have not loved, either. In fact, in turning to this rather painful topic, I think particularly about the familial generation above mine. Many of them made few, if any, friends outside the family, and they didn't even enjoy themselves when they were with the family. Many of these people have now passed away, yet I wonder if they ever knew happiness, or that there was such a thing as happiness available beyond the cold shoulders of each other.

Decades ago, my whole extended family lived close by. A best friend's birthday party on Saturday did not outweigh one's obligation to visit Aunt So-and-So, however dull the visit would be. As cousins, we were constantly made to pose before the camera and smile. (Though interestingly, the same elders asking us to smile for the camera instead often frowned when they themselves posed for family pictures.) Some of us were born at about the same time, and so were raised sort of like twins, and were given the same toys, as if to punctuate a sameness and belongingness that was never really there.

Yet once old enough to be on our own, we spread apart like so many balls of mercury. In fact, my family has not been all in the same room for decades. There are siblings who have not all been in the same room for 20 or more years. If a relative were to visit the town I currently live in, he possibly would not bother to contact me—instead, there would be polite excuses about how they assumed I was busy. The squabbles between this or that person have often been over things that other families get past, and my family members have often forgiven outsiders for worse. (Some years back, an elderly relative referred to Timothy McVeigh as a very nice boy whom she felt sorry for.) Further, the scarcity of my own generation at family gatherings had something of a liberating effect on the generation above us. Some of them stopped pretending to be close and saw much less of each other in later years. Simply put, there just was no love between us—nothing to glue us all together.

Estrangement is a harsh word. In some cultures there are rituals for officially banning people from the family. But for many people in our society, estrangement happens more casually; you just do your best to avoid certain family members. Some people may think: "No, I'm not estranged from my brother; I just haven't spoken to him in 10 years." Or maybe: "I do have to see my brother now and then, but I avoid it, and I make sure I tell him as little as possible about my life." Even without the benefit of a formal ritual, such relatives are, for all practical purposes, estranged. It doesn't say much for the quality of family life when this happens, but apparently many of us give up on the possibility of sharing love when it's depressingly obvious it's never going to happen.

This book is aimed at trying to help the reader recognize behaviors and attitudes that emerge from growing up in a loveless family, as well as how to work—and yes, it takes work—to try to get beyond these limitations. The book makes no promises, as there are no guaranteed, instant ways of setting aside a lifetime of loneliness, resentment, and, yes, sometimes hatred. While my formative years and beyond gave me a great deal of insight into having a loveless family, I have no children myself. However, I am aware that raising a child is no easy task, even in the best of circumstances. Certainly as an adult I see many things from a different perspective. Still, if you think I have no right to comment on parenting, that is your choice. You are free to agree or disagree with anything this book has to say—even or especially if you are a member of my family. This book is how I see things, not necessarily how anyone else sees things. But if readers find the book helpful and can relate to the dynamics I describe, my own challenges will have served a positive purpose.

Whether your family was rich or poor, assimilated, or from another culture; whether there was substance abuse or not; whether there was physical abuse or not; and yes, whether you think it was dysfunctional or not; if you felt unloved, I hope this book has something to offer you. But I did want the reader to know that I am a fellow struggler in learning how to give and receive something I was never taught to give or receive.

One other thought before we get going. And that is the word *unconditional*, as in *unconditional love*. I honestly don't know what that's supposed to mean. It seems to me that *conditional* love is an oxymoron—a square circle. Either you love someone or you don't. You may get angry or impatient with someone, but such feelings can be a form of love. If *love* is turned on and off like a faucet then, to me, it isn't love in the first place. It's a kind of fake niceness trying to pass for love—a formality of etiquette, like knowing which fork to use at a table setting. There is a subtle yet profound difference between a child thinking, "It makes me unhappy when Mom is mad at me," and thinking, "When Mom is mad at me, I *know* she doesn't love me." You are free to disagree, but since this is my book I will simply talk about love, and not worry about whether it is unconditional. Because it seems to me that all love already is unconditional.

About This Book

I am guessing that if you come from a loveless family, you have seldom felt validation for your own thoughts, feelings, and experiences. So the bulk of our time together will be spent trying to identify and validate all those thoughts, feelings, and experiences that few, if any, people in your life have permitted you to do. Honesty will be the goal, more than author or reader being forced to be *nice*—though hopefully you find this book enjoyable and easy to read.

I myself was partially raised by people who were not my biological or adoptive parents, so I know firsthand that not everyone is raised by a mother and/or father. But for the sake of brevity I generally will refer to parents as opposed to primary caregivers, which again I think sounds too clinical and detached. If you technically were not raised by parents, you probably tried to think of these people as parents just the same, even if they rejected the label.

The first part of the book will lay the foundation of what is meant by a loveless family. In part 2, some of the specific patterns and personality profiles seen in a loveless family will be illustrated, along with some of the problems that can emerge from exposure to these kinds of people. Part 3 looks at physical and mental issues, as well as death in the family—things that can and do happen in all families—and how loving versus loveless families may deal with these events. In part 4, we will look at some of the ways we can all try to get beyond the negativity we were taught and have meaningful friendships and relationships, and even create our own families if we so choose.

PART ONE

THE FUNDAMENTALS OF THE LOVELESS FAMILY

1

What Is a Loveless Family?

The loveless family takes many forms. There can be two parents, one, or even none—maybe you got raised by some other relative(s), or got shuffled around in the foster-care system. There could have been divorce or not, and remarriage or not. You may or may not have had siblings, half siblings, or stepsiblings. A family member may or may not have died young, gone to prison, or become an addict. You may have been so abused that your primary caregiver should have been arrested—and maybe even was. Or, at the other end of the spectrum, on the surface everything may have seemed fine, as if your family was trying to imitate one of those perfect families that existed only on TV. Yet something still went haywire and over time there was not much of anything that remained. Or maybe you felt neglected. Basic needs were not met and you may not have been taught proper boundaries for adult life.

Perhaps things got so unbearable that you became one of over a million youths who leave home by choice or by family dictum, and you became one of the 200,000 U.S. homeless youths per year.[1] Or maybe you are the extreme opposite—you are 35 or 60, and you have never seriously dated or built a career because you are still afraid to leave home. Maybe you are a broken spirit still waiting for the confidence that comes from feeling loved.

Further, the loveless family is not limited to any one ethnicity, income level, religion, political affiliation, education level, or lifestyle.

However, there are a few basic things that any or all of these scenarios may have in common where a lack of love is concerned.

Let's say you were walking down the street and a total stranger came up to you and said, "I love you." You'd probably think the person was crazy, maybe even dangerous. At best, you might think he mistook you for someone else—or that she was high on drugs. In any case, it is extremely doubtful that you would believe that this stranger loved you. After all, he knows nothing about you.

And so it is in a family where there is love versus a family where there isn't. To truly love someone you have to know something about who that person is. No one ever fully knows another person—indeed, it has been said that we never fully know ourselves. And even people who are good judges of character can misjudge another person. But when someone thinks you are a certain kind of person—or more to the point, insists that you be a certain kind of person—and this has little in common with how you see yourself or with who you want to be, there is likely to be conflict and a sense of disassociation from that person.[2] Even if the turmoil is always suppressed inside you, it builds over time.

Sometimes people may even refuse to accept factual information about your life. "No, all the doctors who examined you are wrong; there is nothing the matter with you." Someone could be a serial killer, yet his father will still insist he is a good boy. This may be a form of love, but it may be more about the father feeling good about himself than about anything else. If the person has extreme difficulty admitting she is wrong, there can even be bitter disputes about something benign, such as the year he graduated high school. She thinks your life is so much under her control that she is entitled to rewrite your personal history and this can be experienced as invasive.

On the other hand, maybe your family cannot forgive you for something relatively ordinary that in another family would not matter— you won't be flying home for the holidays, you won't loan your cousin-in-law money, you dated someone of a different religion or skin color, you didn't become a lawyer, or you didn't quit college to take care of a sick relative. If your family was extremely strict, maybe you suffered serious, long-term consequences for having sex outside of marriage, or even for using a swear word in the house. You did *something* that signaled you were not who you were *supposed* to be, and this was perceived as unforgivable, or incomprehensible, or both. Even as a young child, perhaps you didn't gravitate toward the things your parent(s) thought you should've gravitated to. She doesn't play with dolls, he doesn't like grandma's famous pot roast—which hurts grandma's feelings and so is unforgivable—she shows no interest in family traditions, he has more personality than his older brother and this complicates the expected order of things, she'd rather play with her friends than with her cousin who's the same age…who the hell *is* she? Certainly not the daughter she's supposed to be. Her actual personality is regarded as coming about due to some sort of brainwashing—it's the fault of some kid she knows—or maybe it's blamed on bad genes or a demon. However, by the age of five she is labeled as a failure because she doesn't fit into the niche that she was assigned to. That she never asked for this niche is beside the point as far as the adults are concerned.

Not surprisingly, then, another common pattern is secrecy:[3] "Yes, I'm very close to my family and we love each other very much. Of course, they have no idea that I'm not really a business executive, or have filed for bankruptcy twice, or have been living with someone for five years, or am gay, or have changed my religious beliefs, or have switched political parties, or that I gave up a child for adoption, or am on medication for depression, or that I self-medicate daily with recreational (illegal) drugs. But we love each other and we're very close." Some people simply are more private than others. And some families do not believe in prying into the affairs of adults. But if you feel that something truly awful would happen if your family knew about these kinds of things—that they would react in some way that would make you unhappy—you may want to reevaluate how much love, acceptance, and trust there really is within your family.

You may feel that it is your duty to stay in touch with a relative. But this sense of duty is likely more about wanting to do the right thing than it is about love. Or if a relative is sick or lonely, perhaps you pity him. But in these or other kinds of scenarios, saying "I love you" somehow does not ring true, even when the words are spoken out loud. You may even experience a physiological reaction—a tightness or sourness inside you for saying something so important that you didn't mean.

Families from certain cultures or religions consider it a sin to say you do not love someone in your family. Even in our progressive culture, parents and children are *supposed to* love each other. Indeed, when loveless families use the word *love* with each other, it often takes on a tragically absurd element—the word *love* becomes meaningless. "Your sister loves you so much," someone might be told, after his sister tried to break a chair over his head. "Just know that I love you," says the father who gambles away the mortgage.

A variation of this is to never exactly say, "I love you." Instead, someone says, "What do you mean, do I love you? What kind of crazy question is that?" Or maybe: "I love her because she's my daughter, but I don't like her."

But whatever is said or not said, just as you cannot truly love some movie star that you've never met, how can someone truly say they love you when they ignore you, belittle you, or are unaware of about 99 percent of who your are?

So perhaps first and foremost, if you felt loveless growing up, it was because you felt that nobody really knew or understood you.[4] Or maybe more to the point, that nobody wanted to. You were taught that you existed merely to fulfill whatever limiting role was assigned to you—whether it was human punching bag, living perfection, or anything in between. Even as an adult, you may find that family members seldom ask or care how you are. And even if you tell them that you're in the hospital facing major surgery, they say something such as, "Oh, but you're fine." Or you tell them you lost your home or your spouse—and they change the subject. You've always been a nuisance, an interruption, and they feel better when they do not have to deal with you.

Thus, when you are forced to be in the same room with family members, you are likely to feel that you are among so many strangers, or even worse, in a roomful of enemies—people who will try to break your spirit out of jealousy, or because they are afraid of something about you that they do not want to know. For if they recognized that you were a 100 percent, flesh-and-blood human being, it would destroy the limited context in which they regarded you.

This may speak volumes about the entire family. There is the familiar old saying, "Where there is smoke, there is fire." If one person in a family feels unloved, it could very well be that other people in the family feel the same way. Perhaps other members also feel that no one wants to know them or that no one really cares about them. Even someone whom you thought was the family favorite may (as an adult) manifest serious problems or confide that she always felt the same way you did. In other instances, the lack of love you feel grows like a weed and even strong relationships stop thriving. A deadly chill permeates the family. If a family says, "We're all very close except one person who's a crack addict, or who's been overseas in the navy for 30 years, or who we just never hear from anymore," there is often more to the story than meets the eye. It would not be surprising to learn that other family members feel nearly the same way as the estranged individual, despite their superficially different behavior.

There may also be someone who tries to get you back into the family fold—not realizing that you never felt part of it in the first place. Usually, these tactics involve guilt baiting, defensiveness, bullying, lying, or a general lack of validation for anything you have to say. Without realizing it, such a person simply is proving how little love there is in the family—how little anyone really wants to get to know you.

Taken one at a time, the members of any small group—in either a family or professional setting—may not seem to be bad people at all. Individuals may appear to be likeable, reasonable, humorous, attractive, intelligent, and empathetic, holding any number of positive qualities. Yet somehow, when the whole group gets together or must communicate with one another, there is a collective sense that nobody likes or loves one another. One factor here can be the unharmonious, inner feelings that the individual participants bring to the group table.

Inner Feelings

In a way, each of us is two people: the person seen by the outside world and the person we keep to ourselves.[5] The more private parts of self are sometimes recorded in diaries or blogs, expressed through a talent or skill one possesses, contemplated upon through prayer or spiritual practice, or shared in bits and pieces with people we trust. These individuals who are deemed trustworthy may include family, friends, professionals, religious or political fellow travelers, or sometimes people such as cab drivers or manicurists. But our inner selves are the thoughts, emotions, and observations that others do not know about us unless we express them in some way.

For family members to love you—as opposed to the of-course-I-love-you-because-we're-related obligation—those members have to know and respect at least some things about your inner self. Sometimes people are delusional, overconfident, under confident, in denial about a problem they have, or simply come to the wrong conclusion. So yes, it is possible to love someone and say, "No, you're wrong, you *can* learn algebra," or "No, you're wrong, you *are* a drug addict." Most people are familiar with what is commonly called tough love—out of love a parent is willing to risk a child being angry with him. But for the words to matter, the person in question still needs to feel that she's been heard—that she's shared, and the other party has listened. Further, tough love involves a realistic appraisal of the situation at hand.[6] It isn't about just trying to punish the child into submission because it's more convenient for the adult.

This means allowing additional information to filter into one's consciousness. It means not assuming that one already knows everything about the person with the problem; as such, the assumption, in effect, becomes dehumanizing. For example, *why* does this individual have serious problems passing an algebra class? Why do so many students today suffer from what is commonly called math anxiety? If, instead, a young person is told something such as, "Look, we work hard to pay for your college education, so stop whining and get an 'A' in algebra," she may feel as though nobody cares about her. That she's just a machine that's supposed to get an A.

Obviously, physical or sexual abuse is the most serious way to make a child feel unloved. Yet a straight-A student who obeys all the household rules can also feel unloved.[7] Even a three-year-old child can sense that there are things that must be kept from the grown-ups. And as this happens, declarations of love start to become hollow; by the time the three-year-old child becomes a teenager the love may seem more like hate—mutual or one-sided—and extremely cynical, even dangerous behavior can be the result. Or on the surface the unloved individual may remain polite to family members, but on the inside he will harbor deep resentments that, despite his best efforts, do not go away.

The crucial and numerous first steps involved in distancing a child and building a loveless environment for the unloved child to develop within include, but are not limited to:

- **The child feels ignored.** Some other family member(s) dominates the family through achievements, illness, bad behavior, or simply through a sense of entitlement. Or the parental generation may think it is the only generation that matters, and so what children have to say—or what they do when not in the room—doesn't matter. Sometimes, too, adopted children, stepchildren, or children made to live with nonparents simply are not attended to as much as biological children are. Their needs are deemed less important, and their sides of the story are dismissed, or never even given a chance to be heard. The child wonders if he matters to anyone at all.

- **The child is always wrong.** When the child opens up about feelings or things that have happened, some parents or older family members feel compelled to tell the child she is wrong, no matter what. The older person needs to feel smarter, superior, and unthreatened. Or the adult has a different agenda for the child that is not nearly as important as the adult insists it is. The child says that Sally is the nicest girl in school, but the adult insists it's really Jenny, because the adult is friends with Jenny's mom. The child's favorite color is green, but the adult's favorite color is blue, and so the adult keeps trying to force blue down the child's throat. The child says he hates another kid in school and is told that he doesn't because it's wrong to hate. It's one thing to teach a child to try to see the good in people, but quite another to tell the child that he isn't feeling what he knows perfectly well he *is* feeling.

This often has to do with an inability to see the child as a separate person. Maybe, too, the older person refuses to believe what the child says because of who else it involves. A woman's nephew says her son hit him on purpose with a baseball and she does nothing about it because she can't accept her son is in any way inferior to her nephew. The child comes to feel it is a waste of time to talk to such people, even if he has no choice and so starts to feel alienated from these people who supposedly love him.

- **The older family member is *always* right.** Respecting one's elders can be important in maintaining family stability. And obviously there can be a great many things that the elders are right about, despite the protests of the child. When a child says that video games are more important than doing homework or that now that he's 14 his parents should let him get drunk, parental sensibility hopefully rules the day.

  But sometimes it's not about the good of the family or the child. Instead, it's the simple fact that some people cannot admit to anyone that they said or did something that was wrong. And such people often are especially embarrassed to admit that they said or did something wrong to a child or teenager. Since children and teenagers do not really count as far as the adult is concerned, the adult may twist things all around—the information *was* correct, the punishment *still* justified. As for a child, for example, catching a grown-up having an affair—the response would be that the kid should just go away and mind her own business.

  The child starts to doubt the wisdom or trustworthiness of such an adult and so gradually stops sharing with him. This can also

create lifetime issues with authority figures that work to one's dis-
advantage in the adult world.[8]

- **The family is in crisis.** The parents are splitting up, someone is
out of work or critically ill, someone committed a felony, someone
is an addict, or any number of serious issues can challenge the
most solid of families. However, sometimes it is not just the situation that matters, but how it is handled. A child may sense—or
be told—that her needs have no place in this scenario and, consequently, she does not want to be a burden. After a while, she
may feel as though everything about her is a burden—that she
is a living burden, and that's all she is—because clearly nothing
about her is worthy of the attention of the people who supposedly
love her.

    Further, young people may be expected to shoulder burdens
that are not age appropriate—things that even adults have trouble
with: "Your father's sick, he didn't mean it when he told you he
was sorry you were born, so you have no right to feel hurt by it";
"Stop playing with your toys and help your sister who has just
OD'd"; "You're eight years old but I'm going to tell you about my
lousy sex life with your mother"; and so on. And in such cases,
there is a strong possibility that the child will never be thanked or
apologized to later.

- **The child is *only* a child.** Some adults think that children do not
notice things or even feel things—or if they do, it cannot possibly
matter. All that matters are the adults' responses to the situation—
the adults' feelings are hurt, the adults are angry or afraid. In
movie terms, the adult casts herself in the leading role and the
child is but a tiny supporting player with a few lines of dialogue.
The adult assumes that the child probably won't remember any
of what has happened—but in point of fact, the child often does
remember. Moreover, when children are out of the room they can
still hear or maybe even see what is being said or done. Children
do not cease to exist just because they have gone to bed or are
playing in another part of the house. In fact, this can be a good test
for revealing just how little a child is regarded as having her own
separate existence: do the grown-ups seem to think she ceases to
exist when she is not right there in front of them? Sometimes, too,
adults foolishly assume that since the child went to bed 10 minutes

ago, he must be asleep. Either way, the adults assume that the child cannot hear them criticize him behind his back, make fun of his problems, have a perfectly good time after yelling at him, or talk about some family matter that is highly disturbing.

- **Overly sensitive family members.** Maybe there is no specific crisis, but the child senses that Mommy or Grandpa is a very unhappy or troubled person, and so the child strives to keep problems or disagreements away from this person. Perhaps the child feels sorry for other people in the family. (Yes, even very young children are capable of feeling pity for older people.) The adult may say, "The moon is the sun," but the child doesn't have the heart to correct him. The child got teased at school that day, but he tells his mother that everything is fine, because she seems so unhappy already. Adults may well have their own secrets that they do not want to burden the child with. But sometimes adults forget that children may be doing the same thing in their own way, on their own scale.

- **Preoccupied family members.** Sometimes adults have superficial conversations with children, but they seem to remember nothing about what was said only a short time later because they were not listening. Nobody's perfect, and it's understandable if a story about what song was sung in kindergarten class that day does not make it into one's long-term memory—especially when one is dealing with serious problems. Still, it is a sign of caring when the adult makes a real effort to consider the child's experiences and observations. Children learn to stop sharing with people who do not seem to care—who seem to have a much more important life than the child, who is blocked from knowing anything about it. A boy a few years younger than his brother may continually be called by his older brother's name—and not by people who suffer from a form of senility, but by people who—or so it would seem—cannot be bothered remembering who he is.

- **The child has a bad secret.** Maybe the child feels he is gay, or is friends with one of the forbidden, bad kids at school. Or maybe the child secretly hates piano lessons, does not want to be a doctor to please Dad, or accidentally caught Dad with his girlfriend and does not have the heart to tell Mom. While many children feel embarrassed by their parents at some point while growing up, sometimes the reason for the embarrassment is quite serious: the parent is mentally ill, or an addict, or always picks abusive partners. In these situations, children often feel that they are the real grown-ups because they know more than the actual grown-ups seem to know. Scorn for the parent(s) can be one of the results over time, especially if the parent acts haughtily, as if he knows everything.

- **Forced affection.** Despite all the ways that cause children to feel unloved, he is told to give Aunt So-and-So a kiss—or maybe even call this person an aunt in the first place when she is just some total stranger with liquor on her breath. Being forced to kiss someone you do not want to kiss cannot help but make you feel cold inside. Adults should know this from their own experience—how would *they* like to be told they have to kiss someone they don't want to kiss? But again, this is only a child, and the child must make adults happy, and not the other way around. This, too, may have a chilling effect on the child's heart. Or maybe an adult yells and screams at a child, and then 10 minutes later is no longer angry, and expects a hug and kiss from the child. In other words, the adult calls all the shots as to what the dominant mood is and the child must play along, even if the child is completely insincere.

These and other inner resentments may result in eruptions of anger and rebellion as the child travels through life. Or the resentments may remain festering inside, just below the boiling point, more or less disenabling him from feeling happy or successful. When he becomes an adult, other family members often continue to belittle him, or—potentially as annoying, yet in a different way—the family members may pretend that the past has never happened and become superficially nicer. But in any case, the ways in which he was made to feel like less than a person may never be acknowledged. If the child dares to bring anything up, either as a child or when grown up, the family member may say something like, "Apologize to your father for being so disrespectful," "It's not nice to talk to your elders that way," or "You have to stop having such a negative attitude." It is also possible that the family member actually *does* apologize, but it is a weak apology, and that family member may erroneously assume that everything is now fine. Though the family member apologizes, it may really only be to make their own selves feel better, and they do not truly consider the pain or stress has been endured by the child or grown-up child. So, in a way, nothing has changed. The child, either young or now grown up, still does not really exist, and it's all about enabling these other people not to have to dwell on anything that makes them feel uncomfortable.

Outward Behavior

Further complicating things is the fact that even the exterior of our lives is subject to interpretation.[9] Actions or appearances that to one person are just fine are not fine at all to the next person. Usually, parents are proud of their children when they do well in school. Yet as a college professor, I have had students whose parents *complain* that their child is doing well in school, because the parents do not approve of all the time it is taking away from their child being able to be with the family. Two boys walking down the street see a box of free kittens. One boy brings home his kitten and his parents say, "There's some milk for it in the refrigerator." The other boy is so afraid of what will happen that he rings the doorbell before going inside, and sure enough is yelled at for being so stupid and thoughtless as to make more work for the family. Woefully, he takes the kitten back to its box down the street. (PS: I was the second boy in this story.)

Behavioral manifestations of lovelessness and estrangement include:

- **Cultural clashes.** A child says or does something that is beyond forgiveness, given her family's unyielding cultural values. Even as a child, the family may alienate her by not showing any interest in the things she likes if these things do not follow family traditions. A child may also experience alienation if the elders do little or nothing to make him a part of the older traditions. For example, if the elders speak Italian, Russian, or Japanese much of the time, and the child does not know this other language, he will grow distant from these people because there is nothing to connect him to these encounters. The elders can't figure out why he doesn't want to be part of something that they are alienating him from—why the child doesn't just want to sit there for hours and listen to his elders speak in a language he doesn't understand.

- **Fear of personal success.** Whether her family wants her to work in the stock room in the family hardware store or to graduate from Harvard Medical School, she may experience emotional distance if she does not follow the family's plan for her. If instead she becomes (for example) a school teacher, auto-mechanic, or dancer, the family may feel that she is beyond their control and so start to distance themselves from her. Since the family does not have a sense of her as her own person, they are hurt and baffled—or maybe outraged—that she exercised this mysterious free will with which to carve her own identity.

  There also may be a lifetime's worth of ill will on everyone's part. The parents resent the child for all the time and effort that they *wasted* trying to make him something that he never wanted to be. The child, in return, may have resented all along the future that his parents tried to force on him.

  Sometimes it is not a matter of becoming a doctor versus a lawyer, but the fact that the child wants to become anything at all. There is an invisible yet tangible barrier built into the family dynamic. No one is permitted to succeed in life beyond what Mom, Dad, or an older brother or sister achieved. If the family is poor, the child must also be poor. If no one in the family is famous, the child cannot grow up to be famous. Still another variation is that someone else in the family is in fact quite successful, but a second or third success story is not allowed.

- **Fear of travel.** Some people never leave New Jersey, Nebraska, Alaska, or wherever they are from. Though it may not be phrased this way, grown-up children may be afraid to travel very far beyond the family nest. In fact, these grown-up children may even be afraid to visit another part of town. Sometimes, this can be because of racism or other forms of prejudice. But it might also be a form of agoraphobia (fear of travel) or xenophobia (fear of the different). And so if the adult moves to some other part of the country—or the world—it is beyond the child's or grown-up child's scope of understanding to ever go and visit, perhaps even if the adult offers to pay expenses. To leave Cleveland, or Brooklyn, or wherever is too large a thought—even if the grown-up child is seriously ill or in trouble. This can make the child feel unimportant to the adult and that the adult is unfair to the child.

The child, as he grows up, may internalize this same fear, and so while he may have always wanted to visit some other part of the world and has the money to do it, he may have trouble actually getting around to doing it. (The day I was to leave for my first trip to Europe, I broke out in a mysterious skin condition that plagued me for the entire journey and disappeared as soon as I got back home. I think it was anxiety over breaking past the obstacle I had always felt was in place that I somehow did not have the cosmic permission to go to Europe—to get beyond those family barriers that had taught me not to achieve anything beyond what anyone else had managed to achieve.)

- **Fear of knowledge.** While some families take pride in the next generation knowing things they do not know, other families feel extremely threatened by this. They fear this new knowledge will make a child harder to control. Also, if a family thinks everything is always about them, then they may be embarrassed that someone—especially a younger person—knows something that they do not. Further, a child's new knowledge might clash with some deeply held family belief. (Growing up, I once had an argument with an elder because my school didn't teach me something that he himself admitted was not true. However, he said, schools should not worry about teaching the truth but about preserving traditional beliefs.)

- **Jealousy.** If a child shows a talent for playing the piano or pitching a baseball, elders or siblings may discourage her rather than encourage her to pursue her ability. If the family members have no exceptional talents themselves, or were maybe never allowed to develop any, they may resent the child and not want her to become someone who makes them seem inferior. The family may make fun of her, belittle her achievements, or go out of their way to demonstrate that she is an outsider to them in order to preserve their own egos or sense of belonging. Achievement is rewarded with punishment, and this can be extremely confusing and hurtful.

- **Double life.** Secrets are a normal part of life and it is not appropriate for parents to share certain information with children. Yet if a parent or child has a completely separate secret life, emotional distance is the all too obvious result. The secret life can be something harmless or it can have serious consequences. But whether a good thing or a bad thing, the secret will make for barriers between the child and the other person. And once a child starts to feel distant from someone, he may also become more critical of the other person, because the lack of emotional loyalty has removed the blinders from him eyes.

- **Legitimate disagreements.** Maybe nobody is mentally ill, a bigot, a control freak, or trying to get back at anyone else, but there are serious splits in the family over things such as politics or religion. Sincerely liberal parents may not understand their sincerely conservative son. After being Methodists for five generations, a family may have difficulty adjusting to their daughter's keen desire to convert to Judaism. What if one child enlists to fight in a war that a sibling strongly opposes? Healthy, loving families can work past these honest differences of opinion. Though there may be some rough spots, the loving family remains intact. The loving family may agree to disagree, learn to joke about the differences, remain open-minded to different points of view, while communicating that they still love each other. But families that are already drifting apart may instead find, in these differences of opinion, the final validation that those who feel the opposite way to them are not worth knowing—and not worth loving.

- **Unacceptable behavior.** All families face serious challenges if one of its members does something truly heinous. If your brother commits murder, is a pedophile, or steals millions of dollars from other people, it may indeed be difficult for the family to hold together at all. Without professional counseling, the family may fall apart, as one person sympathizes with the brother who has committed the act, another never wants to speak to him again, and so on.

  When there are differences of opinion over legal or monetary considerations, the end result might be estrangement: how could she call the cops on her own sister? How could he protect his sister when he knew she murdered someone? Why won't she pay for her attorney? Doesn't she know that she is just enabling her by paying for her attorney?

  If you were a child while older people had these kinds of arguments, you once again may have felt like you didn't matter at all, or you may have been made to take this or that person's side as if you were a pawn on a chess board.

- **Objectification.** What many of these patterns come down to is that the unloved child is not treated as a person—and often does not feel like one. Instead, she is treated like—and may feel like—a thing, an it, an object, a theoretical concept (e.g., the middle child, the only son, the one who's good or bad in math, the one who must become a better athlete, or whatever). This, of course, is also an inner feeling. But it may translate into behavior. After all, if no one in his family thinks he is his own person, why would family members care what they say or do to him? Sometimes adults take out their frustrations over work, marriage, money, or just about anything on children. Rather than confront her boss, a woman might yell at her son, or even beat him. A man not getting sex from his wife decides to get it from his daughter. A sibling teased or bullied at school decides to tease or bully another child.

What these and countless other examples point to is that in loveless families, it is not necessarily about what technically happens, but whether it happens in a climate of love or indifference—or even hate. Faced with a problem, there may be tough love, tears, anger, and perhaps even some four-letter words that get tossed about. But in the end, love is affirmed, maybe even strengthened. By contrast, a family without love might distance themselves from a child simply for using a four-letter word in the presence of an elder. Rules—even if they're made up as the adults go along—seem to matter more than people. Maybe sometimes there seems to be an important coming together. Yet in the end, there is no follow through. For a couple of minutes everyone hugged and cried, but then it was back to business as usual.

There are gay people who come from very conservative, religious backgrounds. In some cases, the parents get past their religious beliefs and say that the child is still part of the family and that they still love her. Yet I have known of instances in which, for example, a young man came out to his family and his father chased him off the property with a loaded shotgun. Regardless of religious beliefs, in some families, love comes first. In other families, love exists only to the extent that it conforms to the religious beliefs—and so, to my way of thinking, it was never love in the first place.

2

What a Loveless Family Does to You

The solution to growing up in a loveless family may seem obvious: why not just make up for it by creating a loving family of your own? Or donate time and money to unfortunate children who might be spared what you had to endure? Obviously these are worthy endeavors. And in addition to being good for other people, you may well feel better about yourself. Yet, oddly enough, even if you've dedicated yourself to your own children's happiness or do a lot of volunteer work, you may still find it hard to come to terms with your own past. Some of the bad feelings may go away, but not necessarily all of them—or what you might feel to be *enough* of them to be happy.[1]

If you really are over having grown up in such a loveless environment, that's great. However, if you only *seem* to be over it, but on the inside it still gets to you, life may be a more confusing endeavor than you wish it were. Some days, weeks, months, or years are more pleasant than others, yet hard as you try, the hurt, fear, or anger from long ago has a way of creeping back up, front and center. In movies, people have a major catharsis that compels them to live happily ever after. But in real life, maybe even something that would seem relatively inconsequential to someone else continues to nag at you. Maybe not 24/7—though on the other hand, maybe it *is* 24/7—but still, the hurtful memory can seem as real as if it's happening all over again. And again.

Of course, some scars do fade over time. Maybe a past incident within your loveless family now seems trivial, or you can see that your elders were right—or at least were trying to do the right thing. Maybe you realize now that you yourself were responsible for whatever it was, though it did not seem that way at the time. Some people have better long-term memories than others, just as some people remember little about the past one way or the other. Still at other times, what seemed tragic in the moment can seem funny in retrospect, or can be viewed later on as an important learning experience. Maybe you feel a tragic incident made you stronger or gave you more insight. Also, of course, the past cannot be relived, so that cognitively and emotionally you may have had to adjust as best you can to many life events simply because you had no choice.

However, wounds can also linger—even worsen over time. Hopefully, we all grow wiser with age, but ironically, wisdom can make a bad memory seem all the more tragic. *Wise* and *forgiving* are not synonymous. It may well be wise to forgive and let go of certain things, but other things may simply have been too painful or heinous to let go of, no matter how hard you've tried. And knowing *more* about life— more about all it could be, and more about how to communicate and problem solve—can make some memories fester over time, because you are that much more aware of something positive that could have happened instead. Consequently, despite therapy, books, religion, volunteer work, an impressive career, knowing lots of people, winning prizes, or creating your own family with someone you love, you may still feel hurt, angry, frightened, or unloved inside.[2] And if this is the case, there are some general ways of thinking, feeling, or acting that you may have adopted.

First, it's important to consider that if you were not raised upon a solid foundation of love, there is a tendency for you to live in a state of uncertainty and insecurity. Even if you are prized for your intelligence or talent, other people seem to be complacent about life in ways that you are not. While others were molded and guided, you were left to flounder and to figure things out for yourself—and what you figured out may have been self-defeating. You may often feel like you are taking wild guesses throughout your life. When something you say or do works out just right, it can seem like a mystical, almost out-of-body experience, because you are so accustomed to not having anything really go the way you want it to. You may even feel a bit scared when things go well—as if on a roller coaster speeding out of control—because there seems to be nothing familiar to anchor yourself to.[3] Unhappiness, not feeling validated, not being listened to, not having your needs recognized by others—all this has become your state of equilibrium. So when you try to break away from your *normal* unhappiness and sense of belittlement, you may experience a kind of aftershock. Even when you win, you still may feel afraid and uncertain—in some ways more so than if you'd lost.

A variation on this theme is an inability to keep compliments, gifts, invitations, and other forms of human grace in perspective.[4] Remember, your *normal* state of being is one in which virtually no one likes you, understands you, cares about you, or treats you with consideration. So if even just one person says something especially nice, the sheer surprise of it seems to make the pain go away—albeit for only a short while. You may find it difficult to eat, sleep, or concentrate because of this natural high you are experiencing. And since you don't have a balanced frame of reference, you might think someone likes you more than he does, or that you aced a job interview when you only did okay.

Perhaps as you get older, you find that these extremes taper off somewhat. But there are a number of areas in which you may find yourself flipping from one side of the coin to the other in a relatively short span of time. This may be because, having never had a firm grasp on life, you feel like someone on ice skates for the first time, wobbling around for something solid to cling to. So as you struggle your way through life as best you can, trying this and then trying that, there may be a tendency to gravitate toward extremes. Good things seem to happen so seldom that what for someone else are crumbs, are, for you, a banquet. Even if good things have started to happen quite often, they still always feel like a novelty, a fluke. So you may go from feeling down to feeling vitally alive in an instant—and then go back again to feeling down—with little in between.

In fact, you, or someone you know, may have wondered if you are bipolar (also called manic depressive), and by all means get tested by a professional to see if you are. But if you are not, it could be instead that your primal life experiences did not train you how to accept or balance the good with the bad, because there wasn't enough good for you to experiment with.

Further complicating things is that you may have erratic responses to other people. Never having had much experience with love and being afraid of revealing too much of yourself to others, you try to minimize your discomfort by struggling as best you can through social relationships. Thus, some people know you as someone who's always serious, while other people know you as someone who's always joking. Some people think you are brilliant and some people think you know next to nothing. Some people think you're the most sensitive person they've ever met and other people think you are the most insensitive person they've ever met. Some people think you are incredibly well organized and some people think you are a buffoon. Some people think you are amazingly sensual and other people think you are impotent or frigid. Some people see you are a mouse hiding in the corner, while other people think you are frighteningly outspoken. You may feel utterly invisible, yet other people may think you have all but devoured the room.

Hopefully you get the idea. But it is hard to maintain a consistent identity when you never know when someone's going to ignore you, or step all over you, or find you unacceptable.[5] Without the music of love teaching you how to dance, you have no idea if you'll be laughed off the dance floor or given a standing ovation. From one moment to the next you're never sure if the sky will fall. But you are ever on your guard for the possibility. Since spontaneity is difficult under these circumstances, even when people laugh at your jokes, or compliment your appearance, or say they admire you, it can feel somewhat hollow. After all, you're not fully connecting. You're doing the best you can, but often that means at best *sort of* connecting as you try to plow through your myriad insecurities. Sometimes even just surviving 30 minutes at an office party can seem like a major achievement. (Years ago, I won a travel prize at the office holiday party, and even though everyone was cheering me—and everyone had consumed a fair amount of alcohol—my dominant feeling from the party was the rejection and embarrassment I felt when someone turned down my offer to dance.)

These lingering bad feelings can manifest in many ways, including but not limited to:

- **Emotional uncertainty.** You may feel things differently than other people apparently do. Something that strikes you as a horrific news story does not seem to bother anyone else. Or something that other people think is of solemn importance means little or nothing to you. Your sense of humor may be hard for people to understand, and while others laugh at a stand-up comic, you do not.

  Real-life or dramatized scenes of people weeping with joy at the sight of a long-lost loved one might mystify you. It's possibly quite difficult for you to understand why seeing a relative—or, for example, a relative saying that she'll go into treatment for her drug addiction—can move someone to tears. If and when you do cry, you may wonder if you're really feeling it or just doing what you're supposed to do. When a relative has good or bad news, you may think there's something wrong with you if you do not have much of a reaction. Exercises designed to help people feel better or connect to others likely leave you cold. If you ever did 12-Step work, every moment of writing out an answer may have been torture, because it didn't mean anything to you.

Yet at other times, you seem to feel things more deeply than others and notice what you feel to be insensitive or rude behavior that no one else does. You know how badly you felt when someone said or did something similar to you, so you are hyperaware of how *not* to treat other people. But since you don't feel comfortable sharing much of what you feel, you keep it to yourself.

Therefore, you might fluctuate between thinking you feel things less than other people do, and that you feel things more than other people do. At times, it may feel like that there is a kind of dead tree living inside you. Then comes a short period of feeling good and suddenly there is a lightness inside you as the pain goes away.

- **Problems with sentiment.** You may well harbor little sentiment for your family and keep few, if any, pictures of family members on display. If someone sends you an old family keepsake, you are likely to see it as a dust catcher more than anything else and give it away, sell it, or throw it in the trash. Traditional occasions that are supposed to make for cherished memories—holidays, birthdays, weddings—mean little to you, and you may even resent having to participate in them.

  Yet since you treasure moments that feel like genuine kindness and acceptance, you may go out of your way to stay in touch with nonfamily members. Your treasured memories may be difficult for other people to understand, because they may be very simple things such as: "I was with my friends in the car and a nice song came on the radio." Or, "One of the best days I ever had was when two different people unexpectedly visited me on the same afternoon. I did not know either one very well or for very long, but in the moment, my heart soared. I could not believe that anyone— let alone one person and then another—would actually go out of their way to say hello to me."

In fact, you may even be able to actually sit down and make a list of the really happy times you have known. And sadly, it may be a short list in the larger scheme of your life.

Probably you've been hurt when nonfamily members don't want to stay in touch after a while. On the other hand, since you are no stranger to the cold shoulder, others may marvel at how easy it is for you to drop someone from your life when they become a burden. You may make it extremely clear to even casual acquaintances that you do not like them—though you may have difficulty accepting that there are few people you actually like. But when you do like someone because they have been kind to you, you may suffer deep insecurity over whether (for example) they will respond to the email you sent them.

- **Uncertainty over social needs.** You do not take any connection to another person for granted, be it a friend or lover. Therefore, when you do feel happy, it's like a special holiday that you remember years later, and you may overreact to it. You may think someone—or many people—are suddenly going to start liking you more than they used to, and you may soon learn that the nice day or email did not mean as much to the other person as it did to you. The other person is much more accustomed to feeling happy—or at least okay—than you are.

  However, since there is a part of you that feels it cannot tolerate any more unloving behavior, at the same time you probably wonder more than most people do if someone is worth staying married to or having as a friend, neighbor, or coworker. Would you possibly be happier simply getting away from everyone? Well, remember how lonely you felt the last time you did that?

  You may have difficulty with the question, "Are you more of an introvert or an extrovert?" even if you instantly answer when asked. ("Isn't it obvious? An extrovert, of course.") Quitting a job or moving far away, you may feel a tremendous relief that the situation at hand is finally over, and good riddance to all of those people. You feel like a character in a war or horror movie fleeing the burning ruins. Then, when loneliness gets to be too much, you may be extremely grateful for the chance to make new friends and present yourself as humble and appreciative—only to get tired of these people, or argumentative when they fail to measure up to your standards, or understand things that you think should be obvious.

You want balm for your pain, but when other people don't offer it like you think they will—or they make the pain worse without realizing it—you can't get away from them quickly enough. Lacking the courage to do this, you might instead tolerate people you don't really like because you don't like being alone.

- **Interactive uncertainty.** When you disagree with something being said, you have little, if any, idea if your response will be too much, not enough, or just right. You wrestle over when principles should triumph over personality: should you risk hurting someone's feelings or disrupting the atmosphere to say something you think is important? If you say it, then maybe nobody will like you...but then, they *already* don't like you as far as you are concerned, or at least they don't like you that much. Since you are hard on yourself, you sometimes wonder if you have any integrity, because you did not stand up to someone, or to a group of people, and instead pretended to go along with what they said. You may also find it necessary to play both sides of the fence—to pretend to agree with two people at work who strongly disagree with each other. Probably you learned how to do this in your family, when two different people were not getting along, and both assumed they had your total loyalty. After all, you weren't a real person to them, so why should you have had any of your own opinions?

    When you do get up the nerve to disagree with someone, you may be so afraid of what may happen that you instantly take it back or try to show that you were saying the same things as everyone else all along. Or you may become strident and lose your cool altogether—either because you couldn't stand stifling your true ideas anymore, or because you feel it's the only way anyone will listen to you. Then, you are frightened and maybe cannot eat or sleep over having done the unthinkable—expressed negative emotion. So again you try to make it all better, even if it means taking back the valid point you were trying to make.

    You also may feel extremely conflicted if, for example, you have a social engagement the same day you have a cold or flu. You may be afraid that if you cancel you'll never hear again from this person(s). So you keep the date or go to the party but are miserable, and people think you are antisocial even if you explain that you don't feel well. Of course, someone might ask, "Why didn't you just stay home?"

You may also have this funny habit of thinking people *should* know you're sick (or angry, or whatever) by the way you're acting, and so you shouldn't have to say anything. You yourself might be the kind of person who's attuned to these things, and so you can't understand why other people wouldn't be.

- **Lack of patience.** Because you generally expect the worst from people, it can cause you considerable anxiety to have to wait on a decision from someone else. As a child, you probably were told by a grown-up, "I'll think about it," but unlike what happened on happy TV shows, after thinking about it they told you no.

  Time causes you anxiety. If you have a one o'clock appointment, should you arrive right on the dot, or be early, or be late? You may be compulsively early when you have to be someplace. Arriving fashionably late to an event can be torture. You can't stand having to wait another 15 minutes. Plus, arriving early enables you to acclimate yourself to the surroundings. This, too, may have been learned in childhood; you may not have liked school, but it was better than being at home, so you always got to school early. But maybe instead you become famous for your punctuality. No one can say you did anything wrong when you arrive right on time. You may also elect to be late to appointments or parties, so that you won't have to spend as much time with people.

  You probably have difficulties with having to repeat yourself, or with someone not understanding what seems obvious to you. Growing up, there was no one who had patience for you, and so you were not able to model your behavior on a positive example.

- **Lack of sympathy and empathy.** Even if you are considered a good listener, or a generous friend, or a sympathetic soul, inwardly you may not feel nearly as much for the person(s) in need as you seem to do. The world can be a mighty cold place, so disingenuous concern is still better than no concern at all. But since you survived your own loveless past, there may be a part of you that feels that anyone and everyone should be able to survive whatever it is they are going through, without any assistance from anyone. You were never allowed to dump your feelings on people, or act out your insecurities, so why should someone else be permitted to do so? If you survived without additional support from anyone, why can't this other person do the same?

You may find that it is harder than you thought to give to someone else the kind of love and caring that you never had yourself. In fact, at times you may even resent the fact that your own children are being showered with love and attention that you never got yourself. This may be especially the case when children get old enough to question and rebel and seem to have no gratitude at all for all the things you did for them that no one ever did for you. If you were beaten as a child, but you *only* yell at your own children, you may be dumbfounded that they seem to fear you or dislike you, the same way you feared or disliked your own parents.

- **A lack of meaning.** Someone else goes to a wedding and thinks, "I can't wait until the couple cuts the cake." But you think something more like: "Why do people do these dumb traditions that don't mean anything?" When everyone laughs and claps when the couple feed each other the cake, you wonder if everyone else only pretends to enjoy it, with a fake smile of your own plastered across your face. The wedding itself is supposed to bring people together, but it makes you feel more alienated due to your own indifference.

  There are many rituals and practices you tolerate because you have to, but they have little or no meaning for you. You don't *care* if the knot in your necktie is straight; if anything, you wonder how the strange custom of neckties came into being at all.

  Things that you think will change how you feel—getting a certain job, having a certain amount of money, buying something you always wanted, or maybe even getting married, or having children—end up changing you less than you'd hoped, even if you get enjoyment from them. Humor—which some people say is extremely important to enjoying life—doesn't have much effect on you, even if you have a reputation for being a humorous person. It is possible for you to laugh uproariously over something and a minute later feel despondent.

- **Life doesn't feel worth it.** When there is little, if any, love in your life, even just going through your daily routine can seem like nothing but drudgery. And in a way, you're right. Just in and of itself, it isn't fun to brush your teeth, and get dressed, and so on. There needs to be something meaningful urging you forward in order for you to enjoy yourself.

Hopefully you are not suicidal, and if you are, you should immediately seek help. (You can call the National Suicide Hotline at 1–800-SUICIDE, as well as check for local services.) But even if you do not attempt to take your life, you may feel as though you wouldn't mind not having to live anymore. If your doctor says you need to be tested for a serious illness, there may be a part of you that hopes it *is* serious—that you can finally just give up and let go. You may also have nights in which you hope you die in your sleep. When you read about someone who has died—perhaps especially someone who had died young—you may feel a bit jealous. You may also feel envious of people who have taken their lives or died of accidental drug overdoses, and you may have a special fascination for them. There may also be an attraction for people in your environment who share your infatuation with self-destruction, especially when you are young.

But you also could be at the other extreme, where you symbolically distance yourself from anything remotely negative. Music or visual images that suggest negativity may literally frighten you well into adulthood. If someone says, "I'm worried that you're not doing well," or "You seem upset about something," you may respond with outrage or perplexity, even though on the inside you know why someone would form such an opinion.

You also may have attempted suicide, and when faced with some complicated situation at work or in your personal life, suicide may be the third or fourth option on your mental list of options. When overwhelmed, you might find a glimmer of comfort in the notion that someday it will all be over. These extreme feelings often diminish or evaporate when you feel you are loved. (Still, it is always good to check with a professional. Chronic depression may be physiological.)

- **A dangerous desire for vengeance.** Many people feel wounded, hurt, and angry for years—maybe for their entire lives—over the lack of love they received as children. In some cases, the pent-up rage is so intense that people go so far as to want vengeance. If your vengeance takes the form of outshining other members of your family through personal achievement or good deeds to others, then the vengeance has served a positive function. If you are determined to take control of the family money, you may later regret it, but these things do happen.

However, if you feel that your hatred is in danger of turning violent, you should seek professional help immediately. If necessary, you can turn yourself in to a local hospital or police station. You should not physically or sexually harm other people, be they the family members who hurt you, or other people on whom you wish to vent your anger. Growing up in a loveless family does not justify or excuse committing assault, battery, rape, molestation, or murder.

Given general conditions such as these, we will now explore some of the more specific role patterns that cause them—the cast of characters in the loveless family. Sadly enough, once exposed to these kinds of behaviors for prolonged periods in your formative years, as an adult you may find yourself acting out against them ("I'll *never* be like my father") or else unconsciously taking on some of these same behavioral patterns. If the latter is true, try not to be too hard on yourself. It's hard to know how to get through life without positive role models, and if you didn't have any, you may just fall back on the role models you *do* know.

In forthcoming chapters, we will explore some of the more specific manifestations of the loveless family and the roles that the members of loveless families may take on. But first and foremost, there is a lack of desire or an inability for people to honestly and vigorously get to know each other.

PART TWO

COMMON SYNDROMES IN THE LOVELESS FAMILY

Are some of these patterns familiar? If so, you are not alone. A given individual—or a family as a whole—may exhibit any or all of these symptoms, depending on which family member(s) are present.

3

The Star Syndrome

General Characteristics

Where there is no love, there is less likely to be give and take, and so there is less likely to be a balance within the family. This leaves the door wide open for someone to assume the role of Star. Narcissism apparently arises from a lack of balanced socialization,[1] and so it is not surprising that in loveless families there is often a Star—or even more than one Star competing for the imaginary throne. Stars want other family members to be mere supporting players, or perhaps even just extras, who only get to walk by in the background. These family Stars assume that their interests, goals, and experiences are automatically much more interesting and important than anyone else's. While sharing with others is important to most everyone, Stars don't know when or how to stop. If the smallest thing happens to them they must tell it to an audience. They assume they are entitled to the most attention, the most resources (such as money), and that rules that apply to other people do not apply to them.

Should another family member dare to question a Star's claim to the Number One position, some sort of extreme response is inevitable. The Star might (for example) hurl insults, lapse into self-pity, or refuse to speak to you for long periods of time. He may also lock himself in a room, as if to intimate the possibility of something awful happening, up to and including suicide. Flipping the coin over, the Star might also confront the questioning party with violence, punching or hitting, or breaking an object. But expect that the slight will not go unpunished.

Stars are stingy in their compliments to others. It's unlikely that anything you do for them will be met with praise, or even a thank you. In
fact, they might insult you instead. They don't see you as a person, so
it doesn't matter what they say or do to you. If you buy them a gift,
it's never exactly right. If you run an errand for them, you ran it incor-
rectly. If you do something that simply cannot avoid praise, Stars will
sulk and brood, or find a way to put you down. If pushed to the limits,
they may do something destructive to themselves or others because
they cannot deal with someone else being appreciated.

Since Stars have to be best in all ways, they may try to control everything about you. If you had a Star parent(s), you had to ask permission
to do things that other kids could do without permission—just to remind you that they were your superior. But siblings or other family
members can also be Stars who want to determine your existence in
terms of how it reflects on them. You may have had to share the Star's
tastes in clothes, food, music, sports, or just about anything—or at least
pretend to. A Star's favorite baseball team had better be your favorite
baseball team, or the Star will keep hammering away at you until it
is. If you like a flavor of ice cream or a recording artist that the Star
does not like, forget it. You'll never know a moment's peace. After all,
if other people know about your own tastes or opinions, they might
listen to them, and the Star will lose attention in the process. If you've
come to a certain opinion about a personal or social issue, be prepared
for the Star to point out where your thinking is wrong, even if it's just
to keep you from dominating a conversation. In fact, it's possible that
over a lifetime, you never say a single thing to a Star that is not in some
way corrected.

Stars feel they must be absolutely certain at all times. Otherwise,
they are not perfect. So sometimes, for decades, they cling to opinions formed in childhood or adolescence. They may proudly boast that
50 years later they still hate some movie star, or still haven't seen some
movie. If they do change their minds about something, there is no
looking back—no sense of having ever been (for example) a Catholic
if they switch to being an Episcopalian. If they hate a certain flavor of
ice cream and then try it and like it, they may act as if it's been their
favorite flavor all along.

Should you wish to adopt a different point of view than the Star
holds, or to let someone into your life whom the Star sees as competition for your attention, you may feel like you are on trial for murder
as you try to explain yourself to the hard, intimidating face of the Star.

He will belittle what you have to say, as if being extremely generous in even hearing you out.

Also, Stars have very little sense that less can be more—that blowing their own horns less loudly might actually *impress* people more than total self-absorption. They have great difficulty comprehending that saying "I'm sorry," or "You were right," might be more appealing and actually win them more favor than refusing to admit that they were ever wrong. And so their insecurities become a vicious cycle. Underneath it all, they are afraid nobody likes them, though some of these people would probably submit to torture before admitting this. But ironically, they're right—because it *is* difficult to like someone who acts the way they do. People genuinely are relieved when a Star is not around. And so, sensing that people do not like them, they puff themselves up all the more and reinforce the pattern.[2]

Though they have difficulty thinking about anyone but themselves, sometimes Stars find it to their advantage to *help*. And I emphasize the word *help* because it's not so much help as trying to make themselves look good. If a Star offers you advice, or runs an errand for you, or tells a joke that makes you laugh, everyone else will hear about it—and *hear* about it—for a long time to come. The person the Star likes to quote the most is himself. No good deed goes unpublicized.

Parents more interested in bragging than actual nurturing and guidance may help foster this inflated self-image.[3] For example, they may lie about the child's achievements or aptitudes to impress others. Rather than say their son is a bum, parents might say he is helping them around the house—for 40 years. If the son is on his own, he may consider it beneath him to have to balance his budget or pay his gambling debts, and so the parents come to his rescue time and again to avoid the embarrassment of having their son in debt. Again, it's less about love than preserving the public image. If the parents have multiple children and one has already been deemed as the Star, they might belittle the achievements of the other children because they don't want to have been proven wrong.

Stars themselves hate any sort of competition from siblings—above and beyond what might be called normal sibling rivalry. In a household in which a parent has an extremely bad temper and is psychologically or physically dangerous, a Star might purposefully get a sibling in trouble, with no regard for how much the sibling will have to suffer. There's also a good possibility that the Star is not the most intelligent, talented, athletic, or attractive child in the family, and so the Star will put down the sibling(s) who is any of these things. If he is moderately good at football, you cannot be *very* good at it. If she is a B student, you should not be an A student. Sometimes this is communicated explicitly, but it may also be an implicit understanding that all concerned simply know.

A Star also often thinks that what his siblings do is completely his own business. He may correct a poem you've written, openly read your secret diary, always betray confidences to parents, throw out something that's important to you, or tell you negative things that other people—including the parents—have said about you, even if it's actually a lie. He'll tell you who you like, and whether or not you're really as in love with someone as you claim to be. Stars may also impose false barriers between other family members and you. They may say that to talk to your mother you have to go through them. As adults, this can lead to bitter conflicts over the care of elders, the handling of estates, and so forth.

People who do actually accomplish interesting or important things often feel they don't have to brag about it. They may even be uncomfortable when people are fawning over them. By contrast, Stars often have accomplished little of substance beneath their veneer of self-worship. Early in life, they may reach the conclusion that they don't have to actually do anything because they are already so superior. Stars sometimes even decide it is beneath them to actually accomplish anything. After all, in order to accomplish something, you have to be willing to withstand criticism and setbacks. So while others are going to college or starting families, Stars may be fully preoccupied basking in their superiority. They may live in dream worlds in which (for example) sitting around thinking or reading, or engaging in some creative pursuit never made public, takes up all their time. Stars might also preoccupy themselves with highly idiosyncratic projects. They have to look up information about another country, sort their books into piles, or make lists.

Stars can have trouble keeping jobs, because they don't like facing things that do not live up to their self-image. They may also insist that whatever they do is the most important thing anyone can do in their workplace or field. If they do keep the same job for a long time, it's unlikely that many people will miss them when they finally retire.

But maybe the Star never works; she lives with her parents or is supported by a partner(s) while she does whatever inconsequential thing she thinks is so important to do. If allegedly staying home to raise children, he will still spend the most time and resources on himself. Over time, the reality of her lack of job qualifications may be too much for her to accept. Sometimes, later in life, the Star experiences a rude awakening of sorts, and does finally go to school or get a job. But again, everyone else has to hear about it.

If dinner took an hour in your family, it's not uncommon for the Star to have dominated, say, 58 out of 60 minutes. Stars are disinclined to ask other people how their day was or what they think about something—they are bad at drawing people out. Also, since Stars do not pause for air, it is next to impossible to get in a word edgewise or to excuse yourself from the conversation, because there is never a little moment in which the barrage lets up.

What the Star has to say can be quite trivial and of little interest to others. It may take a Star seemingly forever to talk about sharpening a pencil. But even when the Star turns to larger issues, what he says can be contradictory, a lie, or just a bunch of nonsense improvised as he goes along. He just needs to say *something*. And while everyone sometimes forgets they already told someone a particular story, Stars can be especially guilty of this. They're so into themselves in the moment that they don't remember what they've already said. The same story might end differently from one telling to the next, because content doesn't matter—just dominance.

When anything involves a group experience—be it a picnic, a wedding, a therapy group, a business meeting, going to a restaurant, or most anything else—don't be surprised if the event becomes a contest of who is the Star. The slightest of snubs—say, a Star is interrupted while talking, or a small huddle of people does not welcome them to join in with enough enthusiasm—can turn into all sorts of backstabbing remarks, and gossip, and intrigue. A Star's entire experience of an event, even if it did not have much to do with him, becomes a story about how much he was featured—or not.

When there is an unavoidable family crisis, a Star's main concern is herself. As long as she feels alright about what happened, so must everyone else. If she does feel a lack, it is everyone else's job to find a way to fill it. And if she does find someone or something that she hopes will work, she is not beyond putting whoever or whatever it is on a pedestal. This may seem inconsistent with being a Star, but remember: it creates the impression that she, above all of humankind, has discovered this great whatever it is. She has found *the* greatest diet book or religion ever created. Her new best friend, therapist, or significant other is *the* greatest person who ever lived. Having found this whatever it is, a Star will either keep it all to herself, or else expect everyone else to conform to her newest belief—though she of course is still in charge. If he and his siblings are orphans, all that matters is that he finds substitute parental figures. His siblings should also think of these people as substitute parents—but their bonds to these people should never be allowed to become stronger than his own.

Giving the devil her due, the Star does help keep lethargy at bay. Loveless families can be lackluster—people with little feeling for each other, that nonetheless are stuck together, are likely to generate little enthusiasm as a group. So while other family members flail about for something to say or do, the Star does at least fill up the silence. And if you are extremely determined to be this fascinating person who gets everyone's attention when you enter a room, you just may succeed at becoming this way, at least to some extent. So Stars do have their charismatic moments. At least some of the time they can be engaging company. In fact, if they stop speaking to you over some minor slight, you may feel a lack in your life, even though when they *do* speak to you they drive you crazy. And by coincidence as much as anything else, some of their advice might be useful, their anecdotes interesting. In fictional settings such as novels or films, someone with a Star personality can be a compelling character, especially if (as is not always the case in real life) he gets his comeuppance by the end of the story. These are people who are more fun watching from a safe distance.

Also, while you probably do not want to be a full-fledged Star yourself, some of her arrogance may have rubbed off on you in a positive way. She certainly never took a backseat to anyone, and even though she may have robbed you of self-confidence, in a strange way you might be able to use her example to get some of your confidence back again.

The Effects of Growing Up with a Star

For better or for worse, a Star might become one of the major figures in your life—even if you do not see him for years or even decades. Stars have strong personalities, and so are hard to forget, even if you do not like them, or in fact hate them. Stars are also very good at devouring all possible attention available, so in the moment you may find it difficult to know how to deal with them. They interrupt conversations, they grab baby photos being shown to other people, and they minimize any good news someone else has by trying to top it with something they did. Despite years of knowing this person—or this *type* of person—they still have a knack for catching you off guard. So any progress you feel you've made as a person may seem to crumble when you see or even text a message to a Star.

It's helpful to remember that word games are only what they are. You may lose the argument with them every time because they are willing to fight dirty—to win at all costs. But this doesn't have to spoil your life, or negate all you've achieved.

Speaking of which, they probably did a lot of damage to your own sense of self, and if you are in therapy, the Stars you have known are likely to be a frequent topic of conversation. You might recall them as sadistic and bullying, and if indeed they have accomplished little with their lives you may well gloat about this more than you let on. This, in turn, may make you wonder if you are a bad person. But how about saying you're human, and leave it at that?

It's possible you've never shaken off all of the things they said or did. Besides suffering from a lack of self-worth and a lack of confidence in your own ability to make decisions, some of a Star's highly opinioned beliefs may have been internalized. Silly as it sounds, you may find it hard to appreciate something that a Star in your life didn't like or approve of. You may have to struggle to give yourself permission to eat something he didn't like to eat, or paint your bedroom walls a color she didn't like. As awful as you found the Star's arrogance, you may find yourself falling back on it in social situations because you have no idea how else to act.

You may also have difficulty crossing those invisible barriers you never had permission to cross. Perhaps you seldom date—or even masturbate—if the Star in your past didn't want you to grow up and have your own life. Or maybe you make sure you do not make more than a certain amount of money, do not travel even when you could, do not buy many things for yourself, or do not keep up with communication technology because the Star in your life did not.

Another possibility is to do the opposite, and make a point of accomplishing all the things the Star only said he would accomplish. However, knowing how out of control the Star may be, you may be reluctant to let him know about all you've achieved. So if you are not in the public eye he may not even know what you've been doing, and your positive achievements become another form of secrecy—like some sort of taboo disease.

Whatever the specifics, you probably have a sense of trying to make up for lost time. You may feel you lost years off your life having to endlessly listen to or cater to the Star. When first living on your own, you probably lived so deeply within the Star's shadow that you barely felt like you had the right to breathe. So you may have taken bad care of yourself, believing on some level that you were pleasing the Star by never being happy.

Also, if you come across as insecure and underdeveloped, you may well attract other Stars into your life, be they friends or romantic partners. You are seen as their latest project, their latest it or thing to mold in their own image. And unfortunately, you may well be easy prey if you lack self-will, or live in fear of speaking up for yourself. As much as you want to get away from Stars and never have to see them again, you were deprived of the right to live your own life, and so you may have very little sense of how to actually do so. You may even think that having a Star to dominate your life is normal, since it's all you know. So despite your best intentions, you may—at first anyway—welcome this person who feeds her own ego by taking over your life. For remember, Stars are likely to have time on their hands, since they don't actually accomplish much.

When you do see a Star from your childhood again, probably little will have changed. Maybe you traveled to the moon, or became a CEO, or won an Academy Award, but five minutes into things the Star is still his old self, and damn if he doesn't find a way to make himself seem superior. It's also possible that, having matured, you see the Star differently now, and despite your years of wanting to rub it in her face, now that she is before you, you find yourself feeling sorry for her.

But sometimes people mellow with age, and if a Star has managed to become a *former* Star, and actually says something like, "Wow, you did it, congratulations," or, "I'm sorry for mistreating you," you may just decide to welcome a dialog. Clearly, this person has been working on improving herself.

On the other hand, if the Star is still very much a Star, it may simply waste your time to try to establish honest communication. If you feel that this person, even if physically absent, is still holding you back, you should consider seeking professional help. But put your own needs before those of the Star. Try to remember that a Star treats most everyone the same way, and so it may not be anything personal against you. But it can be hard to remember this when you are being needlessly hurt.

4

The Bad Example Syndrome

General Characteristics

Since no one is perfect, no one is a perfect parent. There are parents who do everything they can to raise happy, well-adjusted children who grow up to be happy and productive adults. Yet their child still ends up a career criminal, suicidal, or barely able to function. There may be physiological processes at work beyond the parents' control, and in the final analysis no one can completely control or predict what someone else does. Why one life turns out one way while another life turns out a different way can be a mystery that is all but impossible to solve.

Nonetheless, in loveless families, there is not a sense of deep and sincere concern for other family members. So people often spout hollow words that have little conviction behind them, and which have little to do with the lecturer's own behavior or attitudes.[1] People say what they think they're supposed to say. And since the lecturer concerned thinks you're not a real person with your own ideas and beliefs, she doesn't understand when her words fail to convince you. She may even get extremely frustrated with you and express this frustration through rage, violence, or abandonment. At times, you feel as though your entire life boils down to: do I humor this person, or risk her rage by standing up to her?

Many years ago I was lectured by Relative A that I needed to see Relative B again or else I could never live with myself, and so forth. The curious thing was, Relative A had not seen Relative B in many years, either. Nor did Relative B accompany me on the difficult visit to Relative A that led to deeper estrangement—even though I asked Relative B to do so. There was no real connection among any of the players involved, and I'd not yet learned I could stand up for myself. And since I wasn't a real person in Relative A's eyes, Relative A could use me for whatever was trying to be accomplished. Obviously, Relative B didn't honor my status as a human being, either. For when we recognize our shared humanity, we are less inclined to expect that other people should do things that we ourselves are not willing to do.

I was often told that I needed to be kind and understanding toward a relative that scared the pants off of just about everyone, including the people who lectured me. One person who was scared off for life after encountering five minutes of this person's anger spent many years telling me how *good* this person was, and how I needed to let this person into my life. Days after someone apparently attempted suicide—though it wasn't talked about that way—the self-destructive individual lectured me on how I needed a more positive attitude. A recluse, who literally boarded up windows to keep people away, would tell me that I needed the family to have a happy life. People having affairs lectured about always telling the truth. People who constantly bad-mouthed others behind their backs would say it was wrong to gossip. People who yelled and screamed, or threw things, or hit people would five minutes later say how important family love was.

When people are regarded as abstractions they are very easy to lecture—to know what's best for them, and monolithically dismiss them as bad or good people.[2] The goal here is usually not to actually help anything along—indeed, following the person's advice can make a situation go from bad to worse—but to comfort the self with the knowledge that one is making this superficial gesture toward making things better, and to appear to be someone of superior moral fiber.[3]

A good clue to knowing if this is what happened to you is whether or not there was ample room made in the discussion for you to express your own feelings and needs. *And,* if you did so, was what you said routinely dismissed as wrong or a lie, while by contrast, the person lecturing you apparently knew everything?

There's an old saying, "Do as I say, not as I do." However stilted this attitude is, as such, even this dictum probably has no place in the loveless family. Because it means that the speaker at least acknowledges her inconsistency. And in fairness to the speaker, she herself is part of a loveless family, and despite her superficial confidence, she probably fears that she, too, will feel rejected if she is exposed for who she really is.

So instead, this type of person will deny that she is being contradictory and not practicing what she preaches. This process of denial may involve yelling, insults, distortion of truth, even violence.

Also, since you are not regarded as a real person, it is assumed that you never think anything that other people don't know you think, feel anything other people don't know you feel, or make observations of others—including them—and form your own independent judgments and opinions. But in point of fact, especially since you felt isolated much of the time while growing up, you indeed developed an extensive inner self for want of anything else to do.[4] And maybe you became an especially shrewd judge of character.[5] There may have been a million things a day that you noticed but never said anything about, out of fear of what would happen if you spoke up.

There are many common permutations of the Bad Example. In some cases, the Bad Example expects a child to do something that the parental person never did or never had to deal with. Someone who never finishes what he starts tells his children to finish what they start. Someone who never stands up to anyone tells her children they have to learn to stand up for themselves. Someone who never fights for his goals in life expects his children to fight for their goals in life. Someone who's never been in a wheelchair tells his paraplegic daughter to stop feeling sorry for herself. Someone who was never laughed at in school blandly tells a child to not let the mocking of other children bother him. Someone who never lost a parent tells a child who did that she should be happy. A suicidal young person is told he has no right to feel that way because he has so much to live for—or that life was so much harder for the adult at that same age.

In such instances, it apparently does not occur to the older people that maybe they don't know what something is like for another person—especially if they never experienced it themselves. Also, again, superficial, pat answers are used in place of genuine concern, which of course takes genuine time and effort. In effect, by spouting advice, they may really be trying to just make you stop being such a bother.

A variation on this is for the adult to secretly know quite well what it's like to feel bullied, or suicidal, or parentless. But since these memories are painful for the adult, he pretends to never have had them.[6] Having buried all this pain, he may even resent the child for being like him—for reminding him of himself.

Still other people are so self-absorbed that they fail to notice how they are repeating the very same dastardly deeds that were done to them.

I have known people who talk quite a lot about how awful their father or mother was because of some behavior that the complainer does all the time but never realizes it. Sometimes, too, people think that they are entitled to treat others carelessly as a way of making up for their own loveless past. Consequently, what they get in return is more disconfirmation that they are worthy of love.

The adult may label the child who disobeys as the bad or problem child and may emotionally or physically distance herself so that she doesn't have to look into her own self. Again, the message is often that if only this child would completely change or go away, then the family would be happy. Family strife is the fault of this one child. The woman's bad marriage is the fault of this one child. When someone presents himself as not having any problems and pretends to have confidence that he does not actually possess, he is putting impressions above honesty, and so will find it difficult to love.

Another way Bad Examples act out is by having progeny whom they expect to make none of the more obvious blunders they did. The high school dropout is dumbfounded when his son is not a good student. "All he had to do was put in a little effort," the father complains. The woman who had a baby at 16 can't understand it when the child grows up to become a teen mother herself. "I didn't want her to make the same mistakes I did," says the (grand)mother. Parents who were high on drugs for 20 years kick their daughter out of the house for taking drugs. The former suicidal teen cannot understand why his daughter is suicidal. This, of course, may take the form of the parent denying that he ever drank underage, took drugs, had sex (maybe even a baby), or ever got in trouble for anything. I sometimes hear adults with *problem* children say things like, "Sure, I was having sex and taking drugs by the time I was 14, but *that* was different." Or: "I didn't see the point of going to school as a teenager, but that was because I was unhappy." Well, could it be that your child is also unhappy?

With all due respect for tough love, or wishing to make life better for one's children, an absence of empathy can be and often is interpreted as a lack of interest in who your child is—an unwillingness to listen and understand. There are, of course, a great many superstitions and old sayings about children: "The apple doesn't fall far from the tree," and so on. So people once again put the impressions outsiders may be forming above love for their children. The adults want to make it clear they are not bad parents; they just have bad children. In today's world we know that there are genetic predispositions for some mental illnesses and conditions. But some adults do not want to hear this, because they fear it still makes them look bad.

Sometimes, too, the parental figures are not making specific demands on their children but are simply Bad Examples. They cannot control their tempers, they cannot say what they really mean, they cannot organize their lives, they drink or eat too much, they go from one partner to another without regard for the children, they never leave the house, they are hardly ever home, they never clean up after themselves, they habitually break the law—the list is virtually endless.

Sometimes, despite the adult's personal issues, there is still a great deal of love apparent in the family. Of course, love does not automatically make undesirable behavior go away, but when it is present there is the possibility of genuine sympathy, empathy, understanding, communication, and possible resolution. But in a loveless family, the parent who (for example) is openly prejudiced may be dumbfounded when her son gets arrested for a racially motivated fight. When someone is not at all in touch with her own self, it becomes more difficult to harbor or express love, and so a basic connection between one's behavior and its impact on one's children is not made.

Siblings in a loveless family may be Bad Examples by likewise expecting a fellow sibling to do things that they themselves have never done or have been unwilling to do. A woman who takes care of her elderly father may undergo criticism from her sisters for how she is caring for him, when they are doing nothing to help. They do not see her as a flesh-and-blood person with feelings, so they say whatever they want to her. In childhood, sometimes a younger sibling will be held to standards that an older sibling did not live up to at the same age. He may be expected to understand ideas or read books that are beyond the scope of his age, and which the sibling did not understand at that age, either. This can cause the younger sibling to have little confidence in his own mental prowess, because he feels so inferior by comparison.

In loving families, an older sibling may want to show off a little, or genuinely guide the younger sibling. And if, for example, it is a single-parent home, an older sibling may feel somewhat parental toward the younger one, and offer helpful advice or protection. And yes, there may even be some teasing, or times when the older sibling wishes the younger one would stop bothering him. But in loveless families, it may be more about the older sibling proving her superiority, or taking out on the younger sibling all the messages of criticism and inadequacy she received herself from her elders. It may also be that the older sibling is taking on a parental role in inappropriate ways, given how little proper parenting is enacted.[7] For example, formal discipline should not come from noncustodial persons. Another possibility is that the older sibling, feeling unloved herself, wants the younger sibling to stay close by, like a kind of stuffed animal, and so wants to appear superior to kids the same age as the younger sibling. Hopefully, then, the younger sibling will not want much to do with kids his own age.

Older siblings may also tell things to the younger sibling that she is too young to be able to process, or that she should really be hearing from a parental figure—things that would traumatize the older sibling if he had heard them at the age of the younger sibling. For example, maybe an 8-year-old girl is told by her 18-year-old brother that their parents got divorced because their mother got pregnant by a man other than their father. Or that in order to buy the toy the boy wanted for his birthday, his mother had to sell something. Or the older brother tells his little sister about some gruesome crime that gives her nightmares, or some philosophical idea that is beyond her scope of understanding that confuses her. And since there is little appropriate supervision in loveless families—it is too much trouble—the older sibling has free reign to say or do just about anything to the younger one.

In larger families, the sibling Bad Example patterns may be passed along from one to the other, depending on the age differences or other factors. Maybe the oldest does these things to the second or third eldest, who does them to the fifth or sixth eldest, and so on. Sometimes, too, it is not a matter of age. Sometimes the oldest child(s) is relatively disempowered or ignored, and another child, even the youngest, bosses the others around.

Still, in an odd way, Bad Examples can help you to be a better person. You may determine never to be this way yourself. Bad Examples also illustrate quite clearly what it is like to say one thing and do something else, which may provide you with insights into life. And some of the things you are exposed to may prepare you for the complexities that lay ahead. If an older sibling tried to make you read *War and Peace* when you were 12 years old and you couldn't do it, you did still learn there was a book called *War and Peace*, so it did not come as a shock when you had to read it in high school or college. But you may not feel it was all worth the price you had to pay in not being validated as a human being.

The Effects of Growing Up with a Bad Example

You may need a great deal of assistance in trying to make sense of life. You saw a lot that was obviously contradictory, yet received little, if any, validation from other people. So you may have difficulty figuring out how to live or what to believe. Perhaps you turn to a social-action or religious group that is rather extreme, because you appreciate the security it offers in being so sure of itself. Or maybe you tend to be overly suspicious of anything not founded in verifiable logic and reason. And so you do not believe in much of anything. The point here is not your political affiliation, or whether you are religious, agnostic, or atheist. Obviously, these matters are up to you to decide. But if you came from a loveless family, bitterness and confusion may be the driving force behind these decisions.

It is possible that you cling to the Bad Example(s) you grew up with, endlessly hoping for some kind of breakthrough in which the Bad Example acknowledges your own humanity and his or her own errors. Or maybe you do the opposite and decide to have nothing more to do with the Bad Examples. When other family members try to force you to patch this up with So-and-So, you may resent it, and remove those family members from your life as well. Abruptly or little by little, this can lead to complete estrangement from everyone in your family.

You might also have a kind of emotional allergy when it comes to getting any advice or recommendation from anyone. If someone says, "I highly recommend this new movie," even that may feel invasive, and you'll go out of your way *not* to see it. Let alone if someone says, "I think you should get a different job," or, "I know a good doctor who could help you with your bad back." You may think anything other than people leaving you alone is robbing you of something essential. Yes, even if you keep the Bad Examples in your life, or find new ones to take their places. Feeling robbed on the inside is so familiar that it becomes normal for you. Standing up for yourself seems to go against the grain, and in a loveless family you may get zero support, even from people whom you thought would be on your side. Just when you really need them, they decide to pick that very moment to switch loyalties.

It is also possible that you internalized a lot of Bad Example behavior, since you had no good examples to learn from. So perhaps much to your chagrin, you also got in trouble for not paying your taxes, or your own children say the same things about you that you said about your own parents. While there are always going to be things in life that do not seem to make sense, no one taught you to even *try* to make sense of it all. What that mattered was that you were wrong and they were right. So you don't see the problem with going to church on Sunday and then committing extortion on Monday.

There's a booby trap in getting exposed to too many Bad Examples growing up. You may well have every right to complain about having felt unloved, but if or when you cannot give or receive love yourself, you end up accusing other people of doing things that you do yourself. You have every right to still feel traumatized by how your parents mistreated you, but since you do not know how to treat children otherwise, you mistreat your own children. No one ever listened to you, so you never listen to anyone else. Despite your sincerest intentions, you were trapped in the quicksand of Bad Examples, and could find no solution other than to sink down into it.

This may happen unconsciously, but if it does, you may have difficulty accepting accountability for your own actions. No one else in your family ever did, so why should you? When things do not work out well—if you get arrested, or get caught cheating on your spouse—you have trouble believing it, because *normal* means no consistency between word and deed. Though deeply deprived of real love and nurturing, you may come across as conceited or as a snob.

You may have an extremely intense inner life—perhaps too much of one—whereby you live almost entirely inside your own head, because you long ago decided that the outer world was totally crazy. Nobody made sense at all. However, since you were taught not to share your true feelings, you may not be getting any constructive input to change unproductive patterns in your life. You may be simultaneously extremely sensitive because you notice so much, *and* extremely impatient and disenchanted with people. You feel like a thin-skinned cynic. You take it for granted that people are usually at their worst, yet you feel extremely inadequate at coping with this reality.

Or you may have instead developed no inner life whatsoever, because you are afraid of what you may find. Only the outer world, with its concrete objects and issues, is safe territory for you. Any form of therapy or self-improvement is so much hogwash and all that matters are *facts*. In other words, you are more like those people you grew up with than you may choose to realize. You may be concerned about social issues, without any sense of how you yourself treat people. If someone attempts to point out how you may have handled something differently, you become extremely defensive. After all, you had to put up with an awful lot that was inadequate or that made no sense, so why is everyone attacking you when no one ever attacked (for example) your alcoholic father? It is experienced as very unfair, especially if you have made at least some effort to *not* be like your father. Somewhere along the way you reached a threshold of how much advice or criticism you could take, and do not see why everyone keeps hassling you. And again, this may even be within the context of being superficially connected to people or to a group(s), because you are afraid of being left alone to flounder by yourself.

5

The Frenemy Syndrome

General Characteristics

A new word in the dictionary, *Frenemy*, means someone who is an enemy, yet who is also a constant presence in your life that you must deal with. And so on the surface it may seem like you're friends—or in any case, you are used to dealing with each other. Loveless families are likely to abound in Frenemy relationships. The family members are not unfamiliar with the concept that they are *supposed* to love each other, so superficially, people often feel they must make token gestures that signal that they do. But since the family members actually dislike each other, animosity or indifference may come through in a more passive–aggressive way.[1] Even if people are not acting super-close, family members may still at least be superficially pleasant, polite, and supportive, when on the inside they feel completely disconnected and are counting the minutes until they can leave. Or just below the surface the members of the family are fuming with anger and revenge. If there is an outright clash, the participants will still keep seeing each other, despite how they feel.

The sources of these lifelong battles—in a way, they could be called cold wars—may vary. Maybe someone was bullied, but at the time was too young or afraid to speak up.[2] However, the inner resentment festers, and the bullied person looks for ways of getting back as he gets older. It's not uncommon for there to be competition between family members, but when the competition does not rest upon a foundation of love, it's just another ugly competition: who was smartest, was most attractive, should've gone to the best college, should be making the most money, is the better parent...and so on. These competitions can even exist with a deceased family member: "If your sister hadn't died, you'd be nobody." As adults, these competitors may get into protracted money squabbles over wills, estates, the family business, or even result in swindling each other in bogus business deals. Driving the money aspect is a sense on each player's part that there is a deeper principle at stake.

Secrets can also make someone feel like other family members are Frenemies.[3] If you're gay and your family is strongly antigay, then the token Thanksgiving dinner you attend is at best superficially pleasant. There is considerable resentment and lack of trust under the surface. Or maybe you are still dating someone the family does not approve of, or your family has never approved of the partner they know you have. Where there is love, major political or religious differences of opinion can be set aside, or even joked about. But other times these differences rightly or wrongly outweigh family bonds. So the archconservative and ultraliberal siblings barely tolerate each other, but would rather not speak to each other at all. Or perhaps a family tragedy split everyone apart, and the family never truly came back together again, because they never sat down and dealt with the cause of their sorrow.

Owing a huge debt to a family member—which can be money, but can also be, for example, taking in your sister's kids because your sister was a drug addict—can also make for Frenemy family dynamics. When debts can never fully be repaid, the giver may resent having given over time, and the receiver may resent always feeling like less than a full person.

Also, family members secretly may be more jealous than proud over the success of another family member. This may be especially true if they feel that they sacrificed of themselves to help this person succeed. One reads of a great many rifts between former child stars and their parents. This leads to another Frenemy dynamic within the family: having to be polite to someone you feel has ripped you off.

Obviously there are many couples who are Frenemies. If the couple splits up but the individuals have a reason to see each other again, they may bring a great deal of this same tension into the room. And when they stay together, there is an ongoing battle of wills, an unspecified contest that both parties are desperate to win. There also, of course, may be outright fights over specific matters, causing deep rifts in the family that last for years. While such disputes may be enacted in privacy, again it is forgotten that children still exist when they are not in the room, and so the children hear everything that is being said. Taken to an extreme, there are couples who enact their disputes in front of other family members, or nonrelatives. Perhaps these couples get an exhibitionistic excitement from letting others see how poorly they get along. As people tend to tire of being exposed to these displays, the couple may find itself increasingly isolated. So the next-best audience becomes the couple's own children.

Between children and adults, there may be lifelong disappointment over a child's failure to meet the parents' expectations. The child, in turn, may spend a lifetime fluctuating between guilt for having failed and resentment for being expected to succeed in the first place. When parents failed to help when they could and should have—if the child was being sexually abused, for example, and the parents chose not to believe it—the wound may never heal, despite superficial niceties. Sometimes, too, parents actually want their children to fail, as the parents resent never having had their own chance at success.

Caregivers who have fits of violent rage may not understand why, after they calm down, the children keep their distance, or dread seeing this person once they are old enough to move out. There are also parents who say, "Of course I love you," but are seldom warm to the child, yet almost always critical.

In any or all of these scenarios, people often politely suppress their discomfort for the sake of avoiding confrontation—while seething with hatred the entire time. Out of fear—a kind of Stockholm syndrome—you may even go out of your way to be nice to the Frenemy, flattering her and asking for her opinions or her advice.

The fact of being related may compel one or more of the players to make an attempt at becoming closer. Even if you do not see your brother for 40 years, on some level he is still your brother. Adopted children often long to know the birth parents they've never met. So as much as you may loathe admitting it, those family ties do mean something to you, even if you have tried to sever them.

It can also be the case that Frenemies behave differently when alone together than when other people—including other family members—are present. This can be true of adult Frenemies, child Frenemies, or adult–child Frenemies. Perhaps one or more people bully someone else, but don't want other people to know. A mother may not want her partner to know that she hates one of their children. A child or set of children may not want the parents to know just how much another child is picked on. And the bullying does not necessarily stop in youth;

vestiges of it may carry on over a lifetime. If you're about to see or send a message to a certain individual, and you can feel yourself putting on your mental boxing gloves just in case, there is probably a Frenemy dynamic between you.

For one reason or another, someone resents you, is threatened or embarrassed by your existence, or sees you as an easy target to vent their frustrations on. Bullies frequently are people who are bullied by someone else, so it can come as a big surprise when, for example, a seemingly meek and mild family member takes a profound and active dislike to someone else. But people have to do something with their feelings of being ridiculed, and unfortunately one possibility is to ridicule someone else.[4] Growing up, perhaps you ultimately were not so much the victim of your mean older brother as you *were* of your mean father.

Put-downs can be a form of affection—good-naturedly giving someone a hard time can be a positive experience between friends. But put-downs can be purely mean-spirited.[5] Someone knows exactly how to belittle or frighten someone else, and they take sadistic pleasure in doing so. Since we are raised to believe that blood is thicker than water, that of course you love your father, or sister, or half cousin, some people think that they can be as cruel as they choose and it won't matter. The target of their cruelty must still love them, and they are baffled when this does not prove to be the case. So even if someone begins as simply a victim of someone else's meanness, he may start finding ways of fighting back as he gets older, if not directly, then indirectly. If nothing else, maybe you refuse to speak to this person. When it is clear someone does not like you and certainly does not love you, it is reasonable for you to not exactly want to be president of this person's fan club.

But Frenemies may also work more subtly. Besides not wanting to get "caught" hating a family member, Frenemies may have other reasons for not wanting other family members to get involved. This may be because other members choose sides—which can be a nuisance or painful or both—or that their efforts to "help" will only make things worse. They may also try to act as if nothing is happening, but not in a way that signals trying to take the high moral road. Instead, it may seem like, as usual, no one really cares.

So Frenemies may develop ways of taking subtle digs at each other. Maybe one or the other will state a kind of code word that triggers a painful or embarrassing memory for the other one. If at least one Frenemy possesses a sharp, witty tongue—or at least thinks that she does—there can be barbs exchanged to see who can outwit the other(s) in clever insults. Another common pattern is to annoy someone to the point of distraction by repeatedly saying something or doing something that the target person finds annoying.

Again, all of these things can be good-natured fun, but in a loveless family it usually is not, and it can get out of hand. Someone leaves the dinner table deeply hurt or a fight erupts. When I was a teenager, I had an utterly ludicrous argument with another family member as to which of us were more like Jesus! Onlookers were amused and, in retrospect, this should be a funny memory. Yet somehow it isn't. While far from my worst memory, it still reminds me of an empty, burnt-out kind of feeling, a situation in which two people who essentially wished they never had to know each other were grappling with their mutual dislike for each other.

Frenemies love to form alliances and may consider it a total betrayal if you so much as talk to the *other* side. But a Frenemy is just as likely to assume that he has your total loyalty. It does not occur to him that after he is done bad-mouthing the other side to you, the other side might call you five minutes later to do the exact same thing. It's no wonder you feel like a spy sometimes, or reach the point where you want nothing to do with anyone who is involved. Also, since the rivalries may be rather bogus in the first place, you may find (for example) a mother with an anorexic child complaining about some relative for being a bad mother because *her* child is bulimic.

Usually, a Frenemy makes it hard for you to be a casual onlooker—she likes to get you involved, whether you like it or not. But if you are able to just observe from the sidelines, you might feel grateful that at least this is one mess that doesn't involve you. And what your family members are fighting about may be so trivial that you can take a certain amusement in it. You also may become an adroit communicator, learning what to say to this or that person to keep them at bay. And, of course, being involved in an actual Frenemy dynamic yourself may teach you how to be more self-assertive and self-protective. But it all comes with a price. It takes a toll upon your emotions, and after a while you may feel drained or despondent.

The Effects of Growing Up with a Frenemy

At a basic level, you may assume that any or all social encounters can turn into competitions or fights—that at their core, human relationships are antagonistic. If you grew up around a lot of yelling and screaming, you may think this is normal, and not understand it when other people think you are crazy or scary when you lose your temper. You, on the other hand, may be thinking: "What was the big deal? I only raised my voice for about five minutes and that's nothing compared to what I grew up with."

You may also have a way of teasing other people too much. This may have been the closest thing you got to affection while growing up, so even if as a child you hated being made fun of or tickled, you do it to other people because you don't know what else to do. The closer people are to you the more you may engage in these kinds of behaviors.

Also, you may dislike pets. Either you never have any, or you get rid of them when they act like creatures of their species instead of the way you want them to. If you do this, you later may feel guilty for abandoning them, and decide you are a terrible person.

If you have children, you may put them down a lot, or take any comment they make about you extremely personally. You tend to assume that nobody can be trusted, that no one is truly on your side. So if you provide for others, you may take on a martyr complex—even though you hate it when people say that's what you're doing. Working harder than everyone else but getting more flack than anyone else comes to seem normal. You may or may not express the deep animosity this creates inside you, but if you do it's not uncommon for it to come out all wrong. You understate or overstate your case, and people aren't sure how to react.

If you join a religious organization or social group, volunteer for a political campaign, or simply get a job, you manage to gravitate straight to where the action is—the gossipy action, if not the more productive action. You have a keen sense of discerning what the problems are, what questions to ask, and who to suck up to. If there is a guest speaker visiting the group, you may be the one person she talks to at length after making her speech. Before long, you know exactly who hates whom, and for what reasons. People may not exactly seem to like you, yet they find you easy to confide in.

Since familial Frenemies do not necessarily vanish from your life, you experience conflicts when certain behaviors are expected. Do you turn down a wedding invitation from a family member? Do you visit her in the hospital? You may find in these situations that whatever you decide does not feel right.

Though you may have loyalties, you excel at playing both sides of the fence. This can come in handy in politically charged settings—you tell yourself that you are merely spying on one side for the other...only which side is which? You want everyone to like you, even when that is not possible. Yet in another way, all this really is about is not making deep ties to anyone. Sooner or later, you will burn out from all the hopping back and forth, or get caught in the middle of something unpleasant, and move on to something else, vowing that this is the last time you'll do this. The more trivial the matter at hand, the more matters may escalate, and you are disappointed that people can't get past their petty differences.

As you get older, you may grow weary of the whole process and become something of a recluse. Even if you go to work every day, you want to stay out of everything. You go from one extreme to the other.

Even if you think of yourself as a shy person who stuffs about 99 percent of your feelings away, others might see you as confrontational and outspoken. You have a hard time believing that other people can be just as hurt or confused by strong statements as you are, because they seem much more thick-skinned than you. You may try to say something blunt that puts an end to the nonsense, but instead it makes people angry or upset.

You are well aware that the family patterns you grew up with were sick, even ugly. But at times you feel like you have been cursed, and no matter how hard you try, you find yourself in similar situations. However outspoken you may appear, you actually hate confrontations of any kind, and may try hard to avoid them. But somehow, it seldom works out that way.

Your intimate relationships tend not to be 50–50, but to reflect an imbalance of power. There probably are subtle, back-and-forth fights for the crown of King of the House, regardless of gender. Giving in to your partner, or reaching a truce, can feel like you're involved in major United Nations' conferences. Agreeing to close a cupboard door can seem like the compromise of the century.

You may also feel in competition with your children. When your children disobey you, forget what you told them, seem angry with you, learned something you never knew, and in general do not seem grateful or respectful 24/7, you may think they hate you or that your children are engaging in a battle of wills.

If you have been severely damaged by the Frenemy syndrome, you may try to avoid people altogether, and even become a shut-in.

6

The Ostrich Syndrome

General Characteristics

Like the bird famed for burying her head in the sand to hide from troubles, the human Ostrich likewise thinks she can just make all the family problems go away by pretending that they do not even exist. This is similar to what many people call *denial,* but I like the metaphor of the Ostrich, with its large body pitifully still visible while it thinks that it cannot be seen once its own head sees nothing but darkness. A sometimes overlooked aspect of denial is that the denial is *obvious* to other people, by virtue of being able to say, "He is in denial." This means that usually the person—whom we will call an Ostrich—is denying the *obvious.* It's not something you need to be a psychiatrist to understand. He is denying that his daughter who shoots heroin every day is an addict, or that his son who shot and killed someone has serious problems. We are talking about someone who cannot come to terms with that which is staring him right in the face.

I am familiar with someone who has never moved out of his parents' home, and who eventually told his parents that he'd taken LSD hundreds of times at home. Their reaction was one of utter surprise—though predictably enough, this admission did not compel them to take any sort of action. Yet I think about him sitting at the dinner table night after night, tripping on acid, with no one else at the table but his parents—for he was an only child—and the parents never having the slightest clue that maybe something was a little off, or not even admitting that there was the slightest clue that something was not quite right. They just sat there night after night and talked about what someone at the office said at coffee break, or the weather. He was their son, so nothing could be wrong, even when he never did build his own life by moving away, having a career, getting a partner, or raising a family. He never even learned how to drive. But he is, was, and will forever be *fine.*

In fairness to the Ostrich, it is possible that she grew up around a lot of volatile tempers, and so has something of a phobia toward anything that is not superficially pleasant.[1] She herself may also have a bad temper, but somehow these outbursts do not count because she must think of herself as being unlike these other people. Or maybe she was raised by Ostriches herself, and so her frame of reference is that everything must be nice at all times.

There can also be varying cultural standards for what is considered as proper conduct. There are people who all but die of shock if someone expresses any anger at all. Still other people think that even a mild difference of opinion should not be allowed to occur. These Ostriches can make things worse by trying to change the subject or by disqualifying what the other participants are saying.

Ostriches may also have a genuine desire for a happy family. But Ostriches have little idea about how to achieve one, or what to do when problems arise. In a way, they are like children playing house. Someone is a mommy or daddy, someone else is a baby, and no one is supposed to ever do anything out of character. In a sense, Ostriches think happiness is when they are not forced to notice anything.[2]

There are also people who have relatively few inner resources to draw upon. Perhaps the person was not educated much, is not very intelligent, or simply has a weak, defeated nature—for whatever reason. One Ostrich incident I know about concerned grown children and their spouses arguing so intensely that the fight grew physical. The Ostrich just sat there and calmly said, "Can't we all get along?"

Ostriches can also be preoccupied—with personal problems or depression that they are not even aware of. My mother died when I was nine after being sick at home for two years, and over the years, whenever I saw one of her sisters, she would ask me, "Do you remember your mother?" She not only assumed I was too young to remember my mother—a far more convenient thought than having to consider that I did very much remember my mother—but then she couldn't even remember my answer. (And she wasn't that old, either, when she first started asking me.) Or at least she pretended not to remember it, again because it was more convenient for her to do so. Endlessly asking if

I remembered my mother was her way of dealing with the fact that I'd lost my mother as a child. Her conscience was clean. When I was young, I could only bring myself to say, "Yes." As I got older and more assertive, I'd say something like, "Yes, I remember how she'd cry out at night, begging God to let her die." But my aunt's reaction never changed. It was always just, "Oh." Nothing could get her head out of the sand.

At times, Ostriches can provide a comfort of sorts. In the family chaos of estrangement and resentment, the Ostrich remains pleasant. It may be a dishonest pleasantness—it is easier to seem nice if you never deal with anything real—but still, it can be welcomed in the moment. If you have been estranged from an Ostrich, you probably don't have to worry about serious recriminations if you see each other again. Since Ostriches deny anything is wrong, they usually do not take sides in family problems, so—to use an extreme example—if one of your children kills another one of your children, you might get a happy holidays' card from the Ostrich signed with *love*, without further comment, as though nothing has happened. And the murdering daughter, upon being sentenced to death row, may hear a story from the Ostrich about how one of his neighbors accidentally received a letter addressed to the Ostrich, and so brought it over to the Ostrich's home. The Ostrich may somehow even find this to be an amusing story. Funny anecdotes are ones that minimize the life experience rather than speak to its complications. But again, at times this can be a relief.

If it often doesn't take much for an Ostrich to laugh—that someone accidentally put on mismatched socks might be a popular anecdote for years to come—at the same time, it doesn't take much for the Ostrich to be offended. In refusing to recognize much of what actually happens, the Ostrich, despite her pleasant exterior, is usually a highly judgmental person with an extremely narrow vision of what is acceptable.[3] Remember, the reason she is unable to come to terms with having an alcoholic family member (to use a classic example) is because it is *wrong* to be an alcoholic, and so unkind to label someone accordingly.

But in any case, Ostriches give new meaning to the term *small talk*. Like a child unable to count past the number five, Ostriches seem unable to comprehend anything but the most trivial of topics. If you ask an Ostrich how a mutual acquaintance is doing, he might say something like, "Well, his garden didn't sprout many tomatoes this year. He thinks maybe it was the soil." Someone is having a rough time because she cannot find the right varnish for a chair she is refinishing. At the dinner table, an Ostrich may want to know if the mashed potatoes were made from Russets or Idaho. When I mentioned to a relative that I'd visited a neighborhood I'd lived in as a child, his only question was if they still had a particular chain of supermarket across the street. Having not seen him in over a decade, his one question as to the state of my being was if I still liked to eat yogurt.

If an Ostrich is asked to describe herself, she will probably stick to superficial details, even in a self-improvement setting or on an important date. While other people give answers like, "I'm working on becoming a better person," or, "I have problems trusting people," an Ostrich might say something like, "I think So-and-So is a funny comedienne." When asked who in the world they most admire, Ostriches may say something like, "This chef on TV who can make scones in 10 minutes."

Not surprisingly, Ostriches are often exceptionally attentive of babies. Babies are nice and usually easy to make better. Every little gurgle is a potential source of discussion. In fact, they may become worse caregivers as children get older and more complicated. Ostriches long for the days when you were a baby, or maybe three years old. You were so *easy* to love back then, they may tell you, with no regard for the impact of such a statement. But in the meantime, they continue to coo at the babies of total strangers walking down the street, or smile at a very young child.

Ostriches sometimes become the family photographer, taking dozens of pictures of cute little sons, daughters, nieces, and nephews. Any occasion is an excuse for this person to take photo after photo of inconsequential moments. They may even take pictures of strangers sitting next to them in a park—not to produce a work of art, but just for the sake of taking a picture.

Yet passive though they appear, Ostriches can have a major impact in family rifts. Taking no side is, in its way, actually taking a side. They offer little, if any, comfort when the family faces a tragedy—though they may offer considerable empathy if you can't find a rubber band. Children of Ostriches—unless they become Ostriches themselves—usually end up turning to other people for comfort or advice. If they turn to family members, the family members may come to find this a nuisance over time, and resent the Ostrich parent for never dealing with anything.

Yet in their obliviousness, Ostriches are not beyond being rude or hurtful. They may make some nice statement that inadvertently offends. For example, if your partner just died, an Ostrich may tell a (boring) story about a TV commercial that features this wonderful happy couple. They can also get quite testy when little things don't go their way. A fly at a beach becomes a major source of irritation. Ostriches are also very good at being backseat drivers. Since Ostriches want life to be a smooth surface at all times, they take the smallest irritants as serious threats. Usually, though, these threats only concern their own immediate wellbeing.

Whatever their technical religious or political affiliations, Ostriches gravitate toward austere ways of being. They may actually take pride in their plainness. As cooks, they may serve plain vegetables with plain meat and plain potatoes, with maybe plain gelatin for dessert. Faced with many flavor choices of ice cream, they may always get the same thing—which stands a fairly good chance of being vanilla, chocolate, and/or strawberry. In a fancy bakery, they'll order something ordinary, such as a cheese Danish. Ostriches may take pride in always eating the same meal or only liking a couple of songs. If they travel, they may bore people to death with their long-winded accounts of every last detail of the journey—none, apparently, more important than another—or else be obsessed with particular details. An Ostrich might say something like: "I was very impressed with Paris. The traffic lights work so much better there."

Generally, these people have little sense of style. Though often clean and tidy, Ostriches only know how to conform to whatever someone else said is the right thing to do—and probably the reference is far from cutting edge. Their homes may be a mishmash of things that other family members passed on. Not because the Ostrich can't afford something nicer, but because he has no idea what he might actually like. And if it comes from the family it must be good.

If sued or some such, Ostriches usually have little ability to stand up for themselves, as confrontations are not nice. Instead, Ostriches may passive–aggressively complain to other people not involved in the lawsuit. In fact, Ostriches may spend much of their time complaining about other people behind their back, not making cognizance of the fact that they themselves apparently are not the nicest people in the world. If in the hospital with a serious condition, Ostriches may be quite chipper, talking about how nice all the nurses are, or some such talk. But again, Ostriches may pick something small and specific to complain about—that the gelatin is too dry, or their apples always have a bruise.

Though often less damaging than someone who belittled or abused you outright, you may find that in some ways you dislike the do-nothing Ostriches in your life even more. For these were people who could've helped, but didn't.[4] You may reach a point where you can accept that someone who did something terrible was sick, and in your way, you may be able to work things out. But Ostriches remain as oblivious as ever, so there is never anything to work out, and over time they may irritate you more.

The Effects of Growing Up with an Ostrich

Ostriches might give you the distorted impression that everyone is nice—or at least everyone but you, and perhaps those other not-nice people in your life. This may result in some rude awakenings as you journey through life. It may be extremely difficult for you to accept that someone intentionally hurt you. As for unintentional hurts, you may feel compelled to accept them at considerable cost to your own personal sense of self. You may be lacking skills in how to cope with conflict or competition.

Also, you may be ill equipped to survive the conversational perils of the social world. If you have little to say when people are discussing topics more complex than the weather, you may fade into the background at parties, and never enjoy yourself. Or, most unfortunately, you may find that the only way to survive social gatherings is to drink a lot. Only then do you have the confidence to mingle.

You may also feel torn between an urge to be extremely plain, and an urge to break away from this plainness. On some primal level, you can never decide if the *real* you is plain and austere, or wild and complicated. This could lead to living a form of double life: boring office worker by day, easy bar pick-up by night, or maybe even a criminal on the side. Your life has little coherence, because you go from one extreme to another. And when it takes very little for something to be considered bad—when you're criticized no matter what you do—you may decide to go all the way with bad, and cause serious harm to yourself or others. (I once had a long discussion with an Ostrich type, trying in vain to convince him that in some circumstances, lying can be the moral choice. But there was no budging him, even if someone lied to protect a Jew from the Nazis.)

If yours is a rebellious nature, you may go out of your way to *not* be an Ostrich whatsoever. Up to a point, this can be useful, in that you may just create a vivid life for yourself. You will not be afraid of off-color jokes, you will be the life of the party, have exotic affairs, and in general think of yourself as a free sprit not held down by the straight-jacket of society. But there is a risk of going too far. Sometimes people who end up living extremely violent or unsafe lives claim that their families were always so boring—no one talked about anything, nobody ever wanted to go anywhere or do anything, right and wrong were always so clearly defined, and nobody cared when they were being mistreated. So anything even resembling peace and quiet—which *can* be a good thing—is never even considered an option. Life must be busy all the time, filled with adventures (though maybe *problems* is the better word), and you may take many risks. These may include habitually driving too fast, drinking too much, dangerously mixing drugs with alcohol, hooking up with obviously unsafe people, or becoming a career criminal.

When problems do come your way—as indeed they do to everyone—you may have little sense of proportion of the matter at hand. Someone being impolite to you might seem as bad or worse than your house burning down. Even if you rebel against the Ostriches in your past, you might have it ingrained on some level that everyone should have the same nice manners you were taught. And since they do not, much of the time you don't know how to deal with people.

Conversely, since you were raised with a strong emphasis on the superficial, you may engage in some less than thoughtful behavior yourself. If manners have a point, it is to treat others the way you would like to be treated. They are not a means to an end unto themselves. So you may ignore the fact that someone has said she has the flu when you talk to her on the phone for two hours about whether you should paint your living room blue or green. When you get a hostile response for doing things like this, you may not understand why nobody seems to like you. Probably nobody really liked the Ostrich in your past who molded your behavior—including you—but you've picked up some of the same habits.

You may also have a tendency to value objects over people. Perhaps you give much more loving care to your houseplants or collection of snuff boxes than you do to the people in your life. You were taught that it is the small things, not the big things, that matter, and you may be uncomfortable when a situation calls for you to draw upon your inner self. You may try to change the subject, or think it somehow is dangerous—let alone impolite—to delve beneath the surface.

Also, since *everyone* gets angry or frustrated sometimes, you may have a tendency to stuff such feelings, and instead take them out on some person or situation that has nothing to do with what's actually bothering you. Your anger, when it erupts, may catch people off guard, because they always assumed that nothing ever bothered you.

Probably you have little innate ability to stand up for yourself. You've had to learn from scratch how it is that people go about protecting themselves from enemies, putting their own needs first, talking down bullies, and so forth. You cave in very easily to the wills of others, even if you seem like you're a rebellious free spirit, because you have trouble coping with things not being on an even keel.

Essentially, the word *nice* haunts your life. In your world, nice isn't really very nice at all, because it can shut out honesty and integrity. You may feel enslaved to nice, either never rebelling against it or panicking on the inside when you do. On one level, you want everything to be nice all the time, but on another level you can't stand it when niceness obliterates other things that matter much more.

The Clueless Meddler Syndrome

General Characteristics

Some people who believe that everything in a family should be nice do not bury their heads in the sand, but instead actively try to make everything better. This can mean trying to fix a broken relationship, or deciding that you need improving in some other way, whether you like it or not. There are appropriate times to intervene in someone's life, regardless of whether or not they are a relative. If someone has committed a serious crime, and/or is doing serious harm to himself or others, by all means do something about it. But in many cases, the best thing to do is seek out professionals. If someone has committed a crime, call the police. If someone is an addict, call a doctor who specializes in addiction. If someone is mentally ill, call a psychiatrist. If family members are being neglected or abused, call the police or report it to your local family service agency.

But Clueless Meddlers usually would rather handle things themselves—often with disastrous consequences, since they lack professional training and even the ability to understand a situation or to listen. That's why they are *Clueless* Meddlers. It's not about the troubled individual(s); it's about themselves—filling up the void in their own lives through others, as if people were puppets.[1] Once again, it means not recognizing you as your own person who is entitled to live your own life. You can decide what your own relationships with others will be, or whether or not to even have someone in your life at all. But Clueless Meddlers don't understand this—or maybe it is that they refuse to understand.

Since a Clueless Meddler is herself suffering from an absence of love, she may not know how to love, or feel much love inside her beneath her attempted concern. But she does know that somewhere along the way people are supposed to help other people. So to give herself something to do—and become someone that others seek out— she decides to mind other people's business. In a sense, she's actually trying to heal herself. From a distance, it is possible to feel pity for such an individual. But up close and personal, you are more likely to regard him or her as a pain in the ass.

Sometimes, at first, you may appreciate the Clueless Meddler. Especially if you are very young or seeking someone—be it friend, relative, and/or partner—who will somehow make your life better. Having little confidence in your own ability to make life work, and feeling that no one ever understands you, a Clueless Meddler may at first seem like a savior. But when people are put on pedestals, sooner or later they will be taken down. You'll realize that this person really doesn't know everything after all and, in fact, may be more messed up than you are. The falling out in these situations, be they platonic or otherwise, generally is extremely painful.

A good clue for recognizing this kind of person before things get bad is if the person seems to *welcome* idolatry. He seldom, if ever, admits to not knowing exactly what needs to be done, what is wrong with you, or whatever the matter at hand is. If you are an especially needy person, a more measured individual will say, in effect, "You have needs beyond what I can give, so here are some things you can do besides coming to me for everything." By contrast, a Clueless Meddler will be more than happy to take over all aspects of your life, until you feel like you can't decide or do anything without checking with him first.

But maybe you never idolized the Clueless Meddler, and, in fact, resented his interference quite early on in life, because—even when you were too young to articulate it—you could sense that you were being deprived of a self. Having grown up with such a person, as an adult you can spot them from a mile away, and wish they'd keep their distance.

If a Clueless Meddler comes from a small family—or she has exhausted her ability to meddle within her own family—she may seek out stray individuals with no one to turn to, as if adopting a pet. Yet pets often are better treated. Despite what she says—"I love you like a son/daughter"—she will not, in fact, treat you that well, especially if she does have her own children. You are given crumbs, and are expected to think that it is a feast. After all, you are a kind of charity case, a project, an abstraction, and so should be grateful for whatever you are given.

Clueless Meddlers' advice or plans of action tend to be highly idiosyncratic. When it comes to knowledge, Clueless Meddlers usually have only been exposed to what they have chosen to expose themselves to. So their solutions usually feature their own biases and limited frames of reference.[2] A Clueless Meddler may decide to fix someone based on a single book that he liked. And not even necessarily a therapy or self-help book, but *any* book. If she's just read a cookbook and liked it, she may decide that if only you'd read the book as well, all of your depression will vanish. If he is a sports' fanatic, he may be convinced that if only you'd play more sports and be more of an outdoor person, you'd lose all desire to compulsively overeat or shoot heroin. Though society is changing, the general antigay environment has compelled many a parent through the generations to make the child in question do more traditional boy or girl activities so that they become *normal*. Many people find that spirituality helps them with their problems, but some people may become extremely impatient when the practicing of a certain faith does not cure someone's obsessive–compulsive disorder. Lactose-intolerant children are given lots of milk to feel better. Common disorders such as dyslexia, dyspraxia, or Asperger's syndrome supposedly should be overcome through sheer willpower—which the Clueless Meddler is all too happy to teach you. If you have the flu, a Clueless Meddler may decide to cure it by teaching you Yoga.

Sometimes Clueless Meddlers address your most obvious problems, but in other instances they decide that something unimportant to you *should* be your biggest concern. Maybe you are out of work and on the verge of homelessness, but as far as the Clueless Meddler is concerned, your main priority should be your trick knee, whether you like it or not. If your trick knee were fixed, all your other problems would go away. This again may be because of Clueless Meddler's stilted understanding. But it also may be because Clueless Meddlers don't actually want to help you in ways that matter—or admit that they cannot help you. Still another possibility is that Clueless Meddlers don't want you to get better. If you did, then the Clueless Meddler would have no one left to help.

Also, when someone's knowledge base lacks exposure to a variety of viewpoints, Clueless Meddlers are often drawn to groups or books that promise that herein is *the* one and only way to lose weight, make money, cure depression, eliminate back pains, or whatever the problem is.[3] Since the underlying philosophy encourages converting people to this point of view—and *converting* here is really just a glorified way of saying not minding your own business—Clueless Meddlers may feel right at home. The main reason for not being attracted to such a monolithic way of life would be if for whatever reason the Clueless Meddler does not immediately get the opportunity to start telling people what to do. If there are levels of training, a Clueless Meddler probably will not be interested, because he wants to be at the top level instantly. Or maybe she will decide that in her state of superior knowledge, she doesn't need the levels of training, and is already an expert at whatever it is.

One of the ways that Clueless Meddlers frequently cause damage is when they take it upon themselves to fix a damaged relationship within the family. That the Clueless Meddlers themselves have many a damaged relationship within the family is not the point. Why look inside their own lives when they have this *it*, this object—namely you—to fix instead? One thing that every person is entitled to—even, yes, the worst examples of humanity—is to decide whether or not they like you, for whatever the reasons. Maybe the reasons do not make sense to someone else, but they are your reasons and you are entitled to them. But Clueless Meddlers don't comprehend this, because if they did, they would recognize that you are a human being.

So the Clueless Meddler tells a five-year-old child that he must love his older brother who just beat him up. Or the separated couple that they must get back together. Or that someone should leave her partner. Or that you have to attend your cousin's wedding even though you can't afford it and haven't seen the cousin since you were eight years old.

If you try to explain yourself, the Clueless Meddler may call you a liar if he doesn't want to believe that the person you've estranged yourself from actually did abuse your trust. Then, after he has totally invalidated your point of view, he doesn't understand why you want to keep even further distance from the family. Without really knowing or accepting the realities of the situation—which is to say without actually being close to the players involved—the Clueless Meddler will wax poetically about the importance of family. Yet clearly he himself is not willing or able to make genuine connections to family members. To do that, he'd have to be willing to listen.

All this being said, some of the clueless meddling you've experienced may have been beneficial, even if by accident. For example, because you followed her advice, you ended up meeting someone who became important to you. Or perhaps this person saved you from something that would've been even worse. And some of their pseudo-wisdom may have had a grain of truth in it. Also, in the absence of other kinds of support or interest in your life, you may look back and decide that your Clueless Meddler(s) was better than nothing. Maybe you would've totally fallen apart without him or her.

The Effects of Growing Up with a Clueless Meddler

Although you felt that the help offered by the Clueless Meddler was invasive, you may have sought it out once on your own. You may have thought that was the only kind of help or concern the human race had to offer. However, the older you get, the less inclined you probably are to welcome these Clueless Meddlers into your life. In fact, you may become quite standoffish—even if you try to hide it—when someone offers any form of advice that has not been asked for. You may feel particularly peeved when someone gets something wrong. For example, having mentioned that you had a sore leg, someone asks you how your foot is doing. Even if you don't show it, this may open the floodgates of resentment you keep inside for having so often been misunderstood in your needs. People desperate for companionship might make an effort to connect with you, and if you do not want to, you may feel especially irritated by their persistence. Since this person does not know much about you, you can't understand why they are drawn to you, and can only assume it's for an unhealthy reason. (PS: You may be right.)

When people do offer genuine concern, that, too, may be suspicious in your eyes. You probably do not like to be coddled if you aren't feeling well, be it physically or emotionally. When someone says, "Let's talk about it, I care," it can make you want to shut down instead. Depending on the circumstance, you may open up a little, but on the inside you'll resent it. Every now and then, you may actually be glad you took up the offer. But you still may be wary that this new trust will be short-lived.

Since the help and advice you were offered when young often made no sense or was hypocritical, you may feel as though you are spending the rest of your life trying to recover from the insanity of your childhood. So when you are re-exposed to these patterns as an adult, it can feel like a very big deal—that more people are trying to hold you back.

Contrarily, when you do ask for help or for something to go a certain way and do not get it, the disappointment confirms in your mind that people just don't know how to listen. They want what they want, they want you to be who they want you to be, and do not care if your actual needs contradict this. If you say something that people do not comment on, or later credit to someone else, this also confirms your lifelong sense that nobody thinks you are a real person.

However, there may be some people whom you genuinely trust and confide in. It may be difficult for you to articulate why Person A but not Person B makes it into your genuine confidence. But it probably has a lot to do with feeling like Person A respects you as a human being while Person B does not. Perhaps you even have little in common with Person A, yet somehow the two of you click. You understand each other's needs for both privacy and concern, and find a natural healthy balance without having to work on it. But your feelings for people in general may be more negative than others realize.

You may not like knowing that you were talked about behind your back, even if what was said was positive. Something about people discussing you when you are not present brings up feelings of being an object instead of a person. In a sense, you want to make *no* impression on people whom you do not like or trust. The friends you have are people whom you are reasonably confident do not tolerate gossip about you. It's possible that you move or change jobs often—or at least would like to—in order to get away from people whom you feel have misunderstood who you are.

Yet you may obsess about other people quite easily. Having been weaned on Clueless Meddling, you may have been taught at a young age to analyze people and figure out their true motivations, as if you were expected to be a six-year-old shrink. And so publically or privately you do not suffer fools gladly. You may have little patience for the serious problems of others, because really all you want is to be left alone. In fact, while some people fear being alone for even a day, some of your happiest memories may be when you were alone—walking through a park in the fall, watching a snowstorm at night, going for a drive, listening to the ocean, cuddled up in bed while watching an old movie...but alone.

Yet since you get lonely like anyone else, you are likely to be uncertain about just what other people are for. You seem to need them, but when you have them, you often wish they'd go away. As you get older, you may tire of this vicious cycle, and either seek help to change it, or else become a recluse.

8

The One-Way Street Syndrome

General Characteristics

Sometimes we are related to people who do not understand—or refuse to accept—that bonding with another person is a mutual process.[1] Because these relatives do not know how to give and receive love, they create unequal social dynamics in their own favor, and then wonder why they are rejected. If these relatives are not dominant or charismatic personalities by nature, then it may be fairly easy to reject them, or at least think about rejecting them with a minimum of guilt. The rejection may still lead to conflicts, but you are not especially conflicted about removing such a person from your life.

For any number of reasons, a One-Way Streeter does not want to look inside himself, and so it does not occur to him that he may well be guilty of many of the same things that he accuses others of. Someone who frequently stops talking to other people will complain when someone stops talking to *her*. Someone who never sends holiday cards complains that he never gets holiday cards. Someone who beats her child complains about how when she was a child she got beaten. Someone who makes no effort to stay in touch with people complains that no one stays in touch with him.

One-Way Streeters have a way of bringing everything back to themselves.[2] If you say, "I just had a baby," she may say something like, "Yeah, I've been thinking of having a baby, too." No congratulations, no questions—it's all about her. With pretzel logic, One-Way Streeters may also take credit for things they are not responsible for. For example, if a family mutually decides that the living room should be painted a different color, the One-Way Streeter will take full credit for the idea. If the One-Way Streeter was not included in the decision-making process, he may refuse to acknowledge that the living room *is* now a different color. In fact, he may even suffer from amnesia: "Oh, is the living room a different color? I didn't notice." If it wasn't her idea she either pretends to not remember it, or genuinely does not. Because only her own ideas penetrate her consciousness.

These people tend to think that people should come to *them* and conform to *their* expectations in a situation. One-Way Streeters may talk up a blue streak of boring anecdotes and then wonder why nobody likes them. Or they may turn on the TV at a party when it's obvious people are expected to mingle without the benefit of the TV. Or the One-Way Streeter may simply brood in a corner, wondering why no one is approaching them. Others are supposed to agree with the One-Way Streeter, make gestures of love toward them, but the One-Way Streeter does not have to do anything in return.

It can be hard to tell if a One-Way Streeter was never taught certain behaviors or if he simply is incapable of empathizing with the feelings of others.[3] A One-Way Streeter may constantly contact you about some problem she is having—maybe taking up considerable time on a daily basis—and then not invite you to a party she has. When you then decide to cool your connection to her, she doesn't understand why. Or he will say something that obviously is hurtful, but somehow not understand why it is. For example, you invite him to go to a movie with you and he says something like, "No, I'm going to see that movie with my friends." If a One-Way Streeter has just finished yelling at you, she may not understand why you don't want to come over to her place for a barbeque. She has every right to take as long as she wants to heal from the slights she has suffered from other people, but you challenge her abilities to comprehend when you may need the same space in return.

When you apologize or try to make amends, a One-Way Streeter is likely to not accept it unless you agree that whatever happened was 100 percent your fault. Even then, you may get turned away. In fact, he may not even comment on your gesture. However, if you point out anything that he has done to hurt you, he may scream something like, "Well, I'm only human, stop hassling me."

For whatever the reasons, these people are socially awkward, even if they promote themselves as being otherwise. So they are not good at bringing up sensitive topics, or giving you a chance to share your own ideas or feelings. If everyone else in the room understands that Grandpa is drunk so leave him alone, the One-Way Streeter may not get it, and will say or do something tactless that makes things worse. Since all that matters is the One-Way Streeter's self-will, it does not matter how it impacts others.

In terms of the loveless family, this kind of behavior may be enacted because of the superficial, knee-jerk family connections. In his mind, no harm was done because you're his relative, so surely blood is thicker than water.[4] In fact, One-Way Streeters may well say something like, "What's the matter with you? We're cousins, so act like it." As far as the One-Way Streeter is concerned, you love them whether you like it or not. It does not occur to them that to love someone there needs to be some display of loving behavior.

When recalling family history, One-Way Streeters are never self-deprecating.[5] A supposedly funny anecdote from the past never depicts the One-Way Streeter as the brunt of the joke. Beyond the point of good-natured teasing, they may harp on something wrong or silly that you did in the past. But you are forbidden to return the gesture. The One-Way Streeter may also continue to bring up what are, for you, painful memories, and try to turn them into funny stories, or make it all about themselves. If the One-Way Streeter does offer sympathy or empathy, it is likely to be about something you don't remember or about something that never bothered you as much as they want to think it did. Essentially, One-Way Streeters do not realize—or want to realize—that some of what may bother you about your past is *them*.

If they have nothing to show for themselves in the present, One-Way Streeters may live more in the past. They constantly talk about a touchdown they scored in high school or how attractive they looked years ago at a dance. If One-Way Streeters never became true successes in their chosen profession, but came somewhat close at one point, they may talk repeatedly about their 15 minutes of fame. One-Way Streeters' ultimate failure is depicted as being someone else's fault. Indeed, One-Way Streeters' tales may be hard to follow after awhile: "I couldn't get a job because my shoulder hurt and the doctor said I needed surgery, but then I found out I couldn't get surgery, and the doctor said I couldn't see her anymore, and then I needed money because my kitchen caught on fire, and I think the neighbors did it, but they must have bribed the insurance company, because nobody believed me." Or something like that.

One of the more harmful ways these people live in the past is when they create the impression—whether explicitly or implicitly—that they were happier before their children were born. One-Way Streeters' *real* lives were when they were carefree teenagers or childless young adults. One-Way Streeters saturate their children with stories about these fun times or fun best friends from before the children were born. Children often enjoy stories about a parent's youth, but in loving families the children are also given a sense that, however much fun that high-school dance was, the parent does not regret the child's existence—and, in fact, the parent is happier now than when at the high-school dance.

Sometimes parents or other adults treat children by the principal of quid pro quo—every favor one does should receive equal favor in return. This may work between adults, but when parents expect their children to comprehend this notion, it shows that the parents do not understand much about childhood development. Further, if these parents do not want to understand about childhood development, there probably is an extreme impatience present that obliterates any protestations of love. So everything the adult does is supposed to be rewarded with praise; it's all about them. When children shout at their parents, "I didn't ask to be born," it's probably because they are constantly hearing from their parents about all that the parents have sacrificed for them. And the child here has a point. It's simply absurd to think that a 4- or 13-year-old child is going to say to a parent, "Thank you for all those diapers you changed." When children are adopted, or live with relatives other than their parents, they may be made to especially think they must show gratitude at all times, and never make any trouble. When the parent or caregiver also has a biological child, he may strongly favor the biological child either consciously or unconsciously. And unless the disfavored child is extremely unintelligent, she will notice this and start to doubt her own self-worth.

Since they do not look within for life's truths, One-Way Streeters are likely to see the problems of the world—or their own lives—strictly in terms of external factors. One-Way Streeters may be prejudiced against certain kinds of people, or they may be conspiracy theorists. If One-Way Streeters themselves are of a minority group status, they may assume that this and this alone is the only possible explanation for why someone does not treat them as they want to be treated. Prejudice, unfortunately, is very much alive and well in our society. But it is also possible that someone simply acts like a jerk.

A somewhat positive aspect of One-Way Streeters is that they are often easier to stand up to than other kinds of people in a loveless family. Since One-Way Streeters make it so hard for others to be let in to their actual selves, there isn't much of a connection made, and so you may not feel you have anything to lose by telling them off or simply keeping your distance. These people may well respond to your distance with cold silence or rage, but it may not bother you as much as if another type of person were doing this.

One-Way Streeters may also seek retaliation by plotting against you. But even if they do, One-Way Streeters' plots may be easy to foil, because they do not understand the social aspect of life as well as they think they do. Part of making a good plan is starting with a point of truth and logic. If someone starts with the assumption that she is the center of the universe, and has little working knowledge of how interactions generally transpire, her plans stand a good chance of going awry. In a way, One-Way Streeters are like miniature dogs who think they are big dogs. However, do not be too cavalier around them, as a miniature dog can still bite.

The Effects of Growing Up with a One-Way Streeter

You probably find it difficult to miss or feel remorse over a One-Way Streeter, should he or she no longer be a part of your life. Since he gives little of himself away, and since he often lacks a winning personality, there simply isn't much to miss. In fact, you may feel elated for having a weight lifted off your shoulders by no longer having to bother with him. You should not, *repeat not,* cause intentional physical harm to anyone. But if, and when, a One-Way Streeter dies, your reaction might be little more than, "Oh." It's hard to experience a sense of loss over someone who rarely, if ever, gave you anything positive.

All this may cause you to ponder if you are a bad person for feeling nothing but coldness toward a blood relative. You may also feel an emptiness for having a close relative(s) whom you feel little or no connection with. Try not to be too hard on yourself. There may well be many other people whom the One-Way Streeter in question has alienated.

Still, it is sad that a closeness that could have been established never was. Life, of course, can be hard, and it's unfortunate when people who could've helped ease each other's burdens were unable to do so.

You may also experience frustration above and beyond your family life when people seem to get away with behavior that you are not given the same license to commit. Perhaps at work everyone knows that So-and-So is an impossible person, so work colleagues just accept it. But if you dare to express any form of dissatisfaction, you are taken to task.

If your early exposure to a One-Way Streeter(s) was intense—say, your only parental figure(s) was like this—it follows that you may find this influence harder to shake off. It's possible you assume that you'll never really connect with anyone or that you'll never have the opportunity to have your own needs honored. This can lead to allowing yourself to get stepped on and taken advantage of by other people. If you have trouble defending or expressing yourself, you might find some other (misguided) way to acquire a sense of control over your life, such as through food, shopping, or substance abuse.

You may also have modeled your own behavior on this person(s), and so you likewise have little sense of give and take in social interactions. You were not taught by example to say things such as, "Thank you," or "I'm sorry," and your social life might suffer accordingly. In an effort to make friends with someone, maybe you contact them day after day to get together socially, and no matter how many times you are told, "No," you try again. Or you talk about nothing but yourself—say, how your sinus infection is doing—and wonder why you aren't making much of a connection. Since you weren't trained to listen to other people, you have no idea what type of gift to give someone, so you give them the same thing every year, and/or something completely safe and impersonal, like a new pair of socks.

Yet whether you broke away from your family One-way Streeter or internalized her behavioral patterns—or both—it's likely that you worry that your personality is rather drab or unformed. Even if you are a flashy dresser or an easy laugher at parties, underneath it all you are a timid person, and you are uncertain about who you are. Having not received much in the way of validation while growing up, you may feel like a kind of half a person. Some people become more colorful with age, but you run the risk of becoming more ordinary—losing that spark of youth that keeps people vital regardless of their age. You need to find ways of standing up for your own needs and developing all those interests that you keep buried inside you.

In today's world, people talk about having it all, which usually means having a successful career *and* a happy family life. It is difficult for anyone to have it all. It can be extremely challenging to give adequate attention to all aspects of one's life. But, that being said, you may find it especially challenging to pursue more than one thing at a time. If partnered, your mate may find it difficult to read your moods or understand your needs. If single, you may decide to concentrate only on having a career, as you take it for granted that you'll never connect with anyone. Or you may fluctuate between the two and feel conflicted a great deal of the time. A happy solution might be to combine work and family by going into business with your partner. But for this to work, there needs to be a clear sense of what is professional and what is personal.

In fact, you may suffer from a fuzzy sense of personal boundaries. For example, you may expect enormous personal validation from people you work with. Having never received it from your family, you are still hoping to find it somewhere. But what may happen instead is that the people you work with are too busy for all this or do not see it as their job to help you in these ways. You are better off consulting a professional or forming a social network of persons like yourself outside of the workplace. You have every right to become the best possible you. But you need to find a way of going about it that works.

9

The Short-Distance Runner Syndrome

General Characteristics

Not surprisingly, in loveless families people often get along worse the more time they spend together.[1] Why shouldn't they? It's hard to feel close in an atmosphere with little, if any, love apparent, so it's easy for even the smallest annoyances to seem more important than they are. Someone's failing to rinse out the sponge on the kitchen counter is experienced as this person having purposefully set the house on fire. Calamities from 40 years ago can feel like they happened yesterday—there hasn't been much love to foster honest communication, whereby old wounds could heal. This is exacerbated all the more when people literally do not see each other for years on end. Normal progressions through the life course are not even observed, so the person you are angry at is forever 16 or 40.[2] Also, when the players involved do not have confident self-identities, the same situation may be looked at a dozen different ways over the years as people keep switching sides.

So, like inmates from rival gangs forced into the same room, the best that can be hoped for when family members get together is that things go not as badly as feared—or maybe even surprisingly well. If this happens, a promise to stay in better touch or get together much more often is made—but is not kept for long, if at all. Someone who is in a foul mood most of the time is in a good mood for about a day and this signals more happy days to come—though those days never do come.

"I love you," says an adult to a child, seemingly out of nowhere, and after weeks or months of making it clear that she does not. And the child fakes a positive response, wary, with good reason, that this happy time will be short-lived. And so it is. Even when a child must be attended to for being ill or incapacitated, the adults quickly lose patience with caring for the child's needs.

It is sometimes said that to minimize conflict, whenever possible, people should meet in person rather than over the phone, and over the phone rather than through email or texting. The idea is that greater social distance increases the likelihood for acrimony, that people are less likely to be nasty to each other face to face. But in loveless families it is often the reverse. Phone calls are more pleasant than meeting in person and emails are nicer than phone calls. The comfort level increases as the technological possibilities for distance increase. The closer the encounter, the greater the likelihood for explosive disagreements—or, at the other extreme, oppressive lethargy. No one has anything to say to anyone else, or at least nothing of positive value or genuine interest. The participants do better with *more* barriers between them, with less of each other to be exposed to. It can be like meeting an Internet date for the first time: who you expect someone to be may or may not match the reality. Especially if it's a family member you've never met before—like a deadbeat dad—or one you haven't seen in a long time.

In movies or TV shows, it's very easy to solve a family conflict with a hug and a kiss and maybe a few tears thrown in for good measure, with sentimental music in the background. But real life doesn't come with built-in background music. And even when there are the hugs and kisses and tears, in real life the improvement of one's character takes hard work. It can be done, but it doesn't just happen in a few minutes. In the moment, there can be sincere intentions to change a family situation for the better. And this is a nice thing. Even after the whatever-it-was has happened, people *still* would like to be close. Perhaps it even shows the presence of a kind of love. A love that's been trampled on and torn to pieces, but which hasn't completely vanished. It may especially feel this way if there have been years, even decades, since you've seen each other.[3]

But since everyone is still pretty much the same person they were five minutes ago, the resolve cannot hold up against a lifetime of other behavioral patterns.

Also, the animosity or indifference that has consumed a lifetime has a way of sneaking back into one's consciousness. There are adopted people who say they regret looking up their birth parents, or trying to make amends with their estranged father or sister.[4] Over time, one's usual self comes back into play. This can mean that either or both parties don't want to stay in touch after all. Or that the behavior or attitude of either or both parties makes it all but impossible to get any closer.

Short-Distance Runners may also simply say something that sounds good in the moment in order to lessen a conflict—or remove themselves from a conflict—or to create a false sense of love and security. Maybe wishing *will* make it so. "I love our Thanksgiving dinners together," someone who actually hates them might say. "Let's make it more than Thanksgiving when we get together." Because such declarations are not grounded in honesty—maybe there was even a squabble at the dinner table a moment before he said it—the words carry no weight and, in fact, might even build resentment.

A noncustodial parent vows to take the kids to the circus, but never shows up.[5] Children themselves might be treated worse as they get older. If there is remarriage or stepchildren, newcomers dislike each other more over time. Promises made to stop drinking, stop yelling, or communicate better in the future, are kept for maybe a day or a week. As children in the family grow older, they want little if anything to do with each other, and see each other only when necessary—if even then. A parent gets sick—or someone dies—and there is tremendous remorse that ends up changing nothing. A wedding, where everything is pretty and nice and where most people are inebriated, may make family members wonder what the big deal ever was, and vow to stay closer. But before long, things go back to the way they were. A lifetime of resentment and incompatibility doesn't just vanish. Even if you feel grief when someone dies, in a year and a half you may get angry at that person all over again.

While growing up, you may have had parents, caregivers, or siblings who did not keep promises made in a moment of hyper enthusiasm—or perhaps drunkenness. Maybe these family members told you that you could have a dog, or that the family would take a fun trip, or move into a nicer home. These more materialistic kinds of promises could've been stymied by harsh economic realities that the parents wanted to spare you from. But in loving families, perhaps some substitute gesture is made—a hamster instead of a dog—with maybe an explanation to the effect that while the family cannot get a dog just now, maybe someday in the future they will be able to. If the child is old enough, perhaps some incentive can be provided: if she gets an afterschool job, she can have a dog. But when love is in short supply, the parents might instead simply expect the child to understand, and if she gets upset or asks questions she is yelled at. This can have the effect of teaching the child not to want much of anything for herself, because when she does she just makes problems for other people. She may also develop into someone who seldom believes other people.

Other parent–child, Short-Distance Runner dynamics include more emotionally driven situations: "You will *love* your new stepfather," "You and your new stepbrother will be friends," "I promise to listen to you before assuming you did something wrong," "I'll spend more time with you and not all my time with your sister," may be but a few of the many examples that sound familiar. As children learn from example, when these important scenarios fail to materialize—when the sister continues to be the favored child or the stepfather mistreats you—it again confirms that you aren't important enough for the truth to matter. You can just be humored along, and you sense intuitively not to keep bringing it up, as you may lose what little value you seem to have within the family.

Still another general area of Short-Distance Running includes an inability to finish what is started. A parent starts to make something—perhaps for the child—that is never finished. Or it is finished only when one parent screams at the other—within earshot of the child. This can also include household chores such as mowing the lawn, cleaning the house, or throwing away an empty box. Sometimes these latter issues can include a subtext of whose job it is to do what—but the fact that the tasks do not get done, or get done only with a great deal of resentment, shows an inability to mutually problem solve in a constructive, loving manner. At least one person is called a bad person by someone else and obviously this does not foster a loving atmosphere.

Children themselves may be Short-Distance Runners. A girl promises to start doing her homework to bring up her grades, but her resolve collapses after a day or two. A boy promises to get along better with his stepmother, but before long the two people are arguing as usual. When there is genuine love and concern, the parents treat their children like real people, and understand how hard it is even for adults to keep the promises they make—let alone a child or teenager who has not fully matured. And so these matters are not treated as merely superficial: "You broke your promise to me, you never keep your word," and so on. As if a child or teen is an intimate partner who's been caught having an affair. The loveless parent makes it all about himself, rather than considering that the child or teen may need counseling for depression or may have a learning disability.

A Short-Distance Runner can also be a nonrelative who declares themselves to be your aunt or uncle, or who simply is always hanging around. He may volunteer to do something that he does not follow up on. She may also assume that she has a closeness with the family that she does not have, especially not with the children. In fact, the children may be quite puzzled why anyone would want to spend time with their family if they did not have to. So these aunts and uncles seem to be people of poor judgment, and not trustworthy. Often there is a hidden agenda, unbeknownst to the child, or even to some of the adults. There can be an affair going on, or maybe someone is supplying someone else with drugs, or who knows what. Maybe the person is simply trying to escape her own unhappy life. And if the loveless family is too lethargic to stop this person from hanging around, and does not consider the impact that such a person might have, he or she may become a family fixture for a time.

But this type of hanger-on, too, is probably hungry for love and acceptance—so much so that he cannot think past the present moment, and will say all sorts of things that he does not mean. If there is a real family crisis, he will either disappear or else inappropriately decide to take charge of the situation—to the resentment of family members who already have plenty of resentments. When he does not take the hint, there eventually can be stressful confrontations.

Whoever the Short-Distance Runner was, and whatever the person could not deliver after all, if you bring it up you will be criticized, perhaps even by other people. Virtually no one will take your side or say it's understandable for you to feel that way. This may still be the case even when you become an adult—or at least among loveless family members. Maybe your family will say that the real fault was with you. Or that you should've been more understanding. Or that you simply have no right to keep bringing it up.

Someone in my own childhood—an honorary aunt—once promised to take me on a camping trip, and to a place I'd never been to, no less. (I seldom got to go much of anywhere as a child.) I was seven or eight years old. She went on at some length about how wonderful it would be—looking back, she was probably drunk. My older brother was going, too. Years later I found out that the real reason I ended up not going was that her husband was willing to take my brother along, but not me. But rather than say that—or for that matter, check first with her husband—she lectured me, all of seven or eight years old, about Freud's theories of parental identification. She said that my older brother needed a positive male role model, so I should understand that it was important he got to spend this time with her husband. I presumably had no needs, and since I had no needs, I was expected to be understanding, even though I was much younger than everyone else involved.

Also, since a Short-Distance Runner is often oblivious to what is going on, the kind gesture that he does make—or at least offers to make—is superfluous. It takes true commitment to another person to ask, "What does she want for her birthday?" So a girl who hates dolls is given a doll by the father she's seen twice so far in her life. Someone who can drive themselves to the airport is offered a ride to the airport—but the driver doesn't show up.

A positive aspect to having a Short-Distance Runner situation is that it may seem . . . well, better than nothing. For example, if someone dies, another family member might look back and say, "I'm so glad the last time we talked for five minutes or the last afternoon we saw each other five years ago was pleasant." And these people do at least make you aware that there are *possibilities* out there, even if they never fulfilled them.

The Effects of Growing Up with a Short-Distance Runner

You may have considerable anxiety when anything is discussed in the context of a projection into the future. Your wedding is six months away, your boss said she'd get back to you on your special request, you'll be getting a refund in the mail, your friend has said he'd like to go to a movie with you in the near future—who knows what may happen between now and then? Even if you do get whatever it was that you hoped you'd get, you may be very insecure that it will go away. You had a good time at the movies with your friends, but what if they never want to go to the movies with you again? Your spouse will leave you the moment she discovers what you're really like.

Thus, you may have a tendency to overdo, especially when you are younger. You don't just thank the friend for going to the movies with you, you say it was the best time you ever had in your life. You offer to do extra work for your boss for free. You tell your partner that you will give him a body massage every day for the rest of his life. If you hear that there *might* be a party at the office, you ask about it constantly. You are extremely afraid of something that has been promised not happening.

While certainly no one likes to be told, "I thought I was in love with you but I wasn't," or "I *was* in love with you but I'm not anymore," you may have an especially difficult time when making cognitive and emotional peace concerning something that was true, no longer being valid or true. Beyond feeling emotionally devastated by the situation itself, this rejection brings up a lifetime's worth of feeling that no one ever keeps their word, everyone lies, and that no one appreciates you for long. And you cannot help but wonder if it has something to do with you—that you are somehow hexed, or simply unlovable. Even if the word love was never used—if the person only said she liked you or maybe even just that she wanted to see you again—you may have difficulty coping with the notion that someone had the opportunity to select you for a partner and decided not to. A date not showing up feels unbearable. In fact, you may even feel some resentment that someone you have *no* interest in didn't choose you.

You see finding a partner as a means of erasing all the disappointments you suffered, and confirmation that you do deserve someone in your life who is not a constant disappointment for seldom if ever considering your needs. In your quest to find *somebody*, you may have much lower standards than you deserve, and may be willing to tolerate many qualities in this person that cause you unhappiness or even harm. You may be effusive in your praise for another person—even saying you love him—when you do not mean it, just to put an end to having to look for someone. In effect, you risk becoming a Short-Distance Runner yourself, because once the courtship phase is over—even if it only lasted a day!—you will have to live with the reality of a person you do not know very well.

Over time, you may reach a point in which you give up and stop looking. You don't seem to be getting any better with tolerating rejection and so you just don't make yourself vulnerable to it anymore.

Instead of looking for a partner, you may instead look for a close platonic friend(s) who you can always count on, or turn to a group or club. You probably will want to get involved in everything the group is doing and will feel hurt and rejected if you learn that even the smallest occurrence happened in the group without you. When all else fails, you may become a recluse who compensates for loneliness by collecting (too many) things, always being online, always working, or always doing something other than experiencing being alone. Or you may be one of those people who decides that you're simply better off alone because people always disappoint you. If anything, you become *too* accustomed to being alone, and over time you lose some of your social skills.

You may fluctuate between wanting to do everything and be every-thing for everyone, and wanting nothing more than to get away from everything and everyone. This is understandable, because you may take on way too much at once in your quest to feel like you *belong*, and to feel that people will not let you down.

10

The Volcano Syndrome

General Characteristics

Anyone and everyone is capable of losing self-control, and in a loveless family, any of the members—even the ones you least expect—can explode into rage. But the Volcano is someone *especially* known for his emotional meltdowns. It gets to where, when you think of him, you think of him losing his temper. His fits of rage are so frequent and/ or intense that they dominate anything else he might do.[1] A given episode of rage may also contain tears of self-pity, cruel putdowns, denial of any self-accountability, or acts of violence.[2] If the latter occurs, you should call 911 immediately.

Sometimes people can argue or be in a bad mood, and those nearby can go about their business. But not when the angry or hurt person is a Volcano. Like an actual volcano, her rage spills over, and covers everything in its path. It is extremely uncomfortable even to be in the same house with such a person. Even when he isn't erupting, his intensely unhappy mood can spread through the home like a virus. It can feel as though there is no sunlight left anywhere in the world. Whether acting out or unusually quiet, he seems detached from everyday reality—and he probably is. His sudden and fleeting good moods may seem sad and confusing over time, and after a while you may feel you need to give up on this person in order to maintain any sense of self.[3]

It may also become emotionally or physically exhausting after a while to have to say and do things with one eye on the omnipresent Volcano. You can't just say, "We're out of milk," or, "I think I'll go for a walk," because it might spark an attack from the Volcano. There doesn't have to be an actual major issue to set off the Volcano in your life. Again, like an actual volcano, his eruptions may be unpredictable.

Those familiar with the patterns of domestic violence already know that there is a building toward the eruption, the eruption itself, and then remorse and promises to never do it again. A brief period of what is called a *honeymoon* follows, in which things seem to be better.[4] But soon enough, the rage starts to build, and the cycle repeats itself. I submit herein that this same cycle can occur in other family (or work) situations. There may or may not be the violence that is associated with spousal abuse, but there will be a build up to rage, and a honeymoon-like aftermath. And, again like domestic violence, the cycle may become more rapid over time.

Email and texting can allow this cycle to happen from a safer distance, though emotionally a nasty email or text message can sting pretty badly.[5] There can also be a trail left behind that shows how a conversation went from, say, asking a question, to more and more rage. An unintended consequence of e-communication is that it can enhance the possibility and pace of emotional explosions. If you e-communicate with a Volcano, you may literally spend hours composing a short message, in the vain hope of not eliciting the rage you know is coming.

Sensible people strive to keep a safe distance from such a person. But this may be easier said than done. If as a child either or both of your parents were Volcanoes—or one or more siblings was—you may have felt pretty much stuck. Perhaps you tried to stay away from home as much as possible. It simply made good sense not to jump into the angry jaws of a Volcano. Yet you may have been forced to spend more time at home because of this. Volcanoes feel slighted extremely easily, and so you were told you had to stay home and be with the family. You may have tried to calm the person down, logically explain why there was no reason to get so upset, fight back, or you may have just sat there, scared out of your mind. Yet you may also have found that whatever you tried to do, it never worked.[6] Someone spoiling for a fight does not listen to reason. She will maneuver the situation—lying whenever necessary—to keep it what she wants it to be. However verbally dexterous you are, and even if you are more intelligent than the Volcano, he manages to trap you every time. She hears only what she wants to hear—or, if an email, she reads only what she wants to read—and even if the farthest thing from your mind is what you are being accused of, you feel cornered. You may try in vain to defend yourself, but that probably just digs you deeper into the hole.

Coming from a loveless family, you may especially want honesty and integrity in your life, so it may be extremely difficult to ignore a Volcano once the accusations start getting hurled. In the moment, you may feel that to have anything of yourself left at all you need to explain yourself or strike back—especially if you lacked the ability to do so as a child.

Yet, hard as it is to do, you may be better off simply ignoring the Volcano. As an adult you do not have to see this person socially, and if you work with such a person you can seek a professional intervention or stay away from the Volcano as much as possible. (You may also consider asking for a transfer or looking for a different job.)

Ironically, keeping a safe distance may make the Volcano worse than ever. Since underneath it all he feels that nobody wants to be around him, your cold shoulder confirms his worst fear. He may go out of his way to re-ingratiate himself to you. Then you are faced with giving him another chance—and you know how that's going to end up—or continuing to ignore him as much as possible, which may be awkward to pull off, depending on the situation.

But what the Volcano doesn't understand is that she is her own worst enemy. She desperately wants to feel a connection to others. But since she is incapable of considering anyone's point of view but her own, she has no idea how to build a mutual friendship or intimate relationship. Somehow, her bad temper does not count, as far as she is concerned. If you ask her how she sees herself, she probably will be full of self-praise, and describe herself as a very kind person, even a selfless one.

In fact, when his rages are juxtaposed against other things he says or does, he seems to be an exceptionally contradictory person who makes no sense. And if you value truth and honesty, it may be extremely difficult not to obsess about him. Years or even decades after the fact, you may still play back an incident in your mind, thinking about what you *should've* said but lacked the courage to say. However, it could be that what you did say or do was a wiser choice, even if it was a less satisfying one. Volcanoes usually have serious mental conditions, a terminal and/or painful physical condition, or are substance abusers, and those magic words you wished you said probably would've made no difference. If you find yourself becoming self-abusive over this person, are unable to let go of the past, or fantasize acts of violence against him, you should seek professional help.

In the abstract, what upsets her so terribly may be a function of misinformation or a distorted worldview. So you think that people *should* be able to stand up to the Volcano. Yet even when another family member, work associate, or friend says that he will stand up for you and will give this volcanic person a good piece of his mind, he may end up chickening out. Once face-to-face with the Volcano, he doesn't want the latest lava-like round of hurtful remarks directed at him. So instead of saying something like, "Your behavior toward Mary is unacceptable," as he promised to do, he says something more like, "You and Mary need to sit down and have a talk about why you can't get along with each other." This distorts things all the more, because unless you are hiding from the truth yourself, you probably did nothing to deserve the hurt that was heaped upon you.

Also, others may insist that the Volcano in your life is not as bad as you are making her out to be. This could be another variation on the Stockholm syndrome, in which people want to please their abusers. It may also be that others have difficulty acknowledging their own negative feelings toward anyone or that they feel they must remain loyal to this person for some reason. Besides a belief that family must stick together no matter what, this loyalty may be based on other forms of shared identity. Some men always stand up for other men and some women always stand up for other women. There also may be an immutable loyalty based on shared ethnicity, shared sexual orientation, shared generation, shared political views, shared physical condition...shared any number of things that may compel the person you are talking to not to do anything to protect you, or even to admit that your point of view is valid. Sometimes, too, people do not reason things out much, and so they confuse pitying someone or finding her fun to gossip with as being a *good* person.

In fact, one form of loyalty or another may result in the blame being shifted to you. Other family members may insist that the person in question is a good boy, and so you are lying, or you must've done something to him to make him so upset. Other family members may also appeal to your sense of charity and forgiveness, as if your own needs do not count at all. When someone says, "It isn't that bad," or, "He's just having a bad reaction to his meds," it could very well be that this person does not have to live with the Volcano like you do. Or you may be offered innocuous advice: "Just don't let it bother you," or, "You're only hurting yourself by letting him get to you."

Many people feel that their lives are shattered by these kinds of people, so it is difficult to come up with much to say about them that is positive. However, in some ways a Volcano may have shown you that it *is* possible to stand up for yourself—however inappropriately the

Volcano herself did this. A Volcano may also have inspired alliances of a sort to form. Even in a loveless family, you and another family member can look back and agree that So-and-So was truly a monster.

The Effects of Growing Up with a Volcano

As much as you promise yourself you will never act like a Volcano, the role model this person provided you with may have rubbed off more than you care to admit. Even if you stuff your anger and rage away, and always act nice, and never make trouble for other people, underneath it all you may have an extremely short fuse. All that unexpressed anger may then turn itself on you. Rather than stand up to people, you turn to drugs and alcohol to self-medicate. Or the pressure reaches the breaking point, and you turn from Dr. Jekyll to Mr. or Ms. Hyde. You were hardly taught how to cultivate patience, plus you may feel that you've been through enough rage in your life already. So when confronted with something unpleasant, you erupt in rage yourself out of sheer frustration. Or you continue to stuff it away even more. This can result in an increasing inability to socially relate to anyone ("Can't they see how angry I am?") and/or a misdirection of your rage onto yourself. You may abuse yourself in any number of ways, up to and including an attempt at suicide. Again call 1–800-SUICIDE if you are having suicidal thoughts.

If you do occasionally lose your cool, you are probably frightened afterwards. Even if you expressed anger or disappointment through an email, you are filled with genuine terror when checking you email for the reply. Somehow, everyone but you seems to have the right to get angry. Typically, you end up apologizing not only for getting emotional, but for even raising the issue in the first place. After all, you believe that you do not have the same rights as other people. So if you express *any* anger at all, something bad will happen. Even if the Volcano from your childhood has died, it's as though his rage will mystically get transferred to another person, and you'll feel that awful way all over again. While supposedly it feels good to let out your negativity, you may feel the opposite is true: anger on your part just leads to more anger, or else fear. A nasty conversation or email with someone at work may make it hard for you to eat or sleep.

Since Volcanoes are master manipulators, they are very good at making you feel guilty when you refuse to speak to them. They may also do something extra nice for you or become vulnerable, like a small child, in your presence. Over time, when you give in yet again, this surrender may be increasingly insincere on your part, and in your own way you may become as bitter as the Volcano is.

Especially if you had to grow up in the shadow of a Volcano, you may deeply resent having to go through it all again at work, or within the family you create for yourself. You may feel as though you are cursed—that while other people get to enjoy themselves, you always end up with people who make life ugly.

Yet whether you strive to never be a Volcano or are one at least some of the time, you probably have deeply confused feelings over your right to express yourself. In a kind of movie in your mind, maybe you are always putting people in their place. But in real life—surprise!— people often fight back. They do not always retreat like frightened children. So angry as you are, your opponent may out-anger you. The other person may also point out that you came to an incorrect conclusion. Might does not make right—even if it is coming from you.

Also, because of the connections you have made in your mind, if someone loses her temper with you, you feel it is an unbearable torture. So it may be easy to boss you around even as an adult. An eruption of temper by itself does not physically hurt another person, yet it is amazing how much it can hurt in other ways. Therefore, you may fall back on skills developed long ago to say things very carefully to someone, to humor him or offer false praise, rather than risk his ire.

Further, you may get angry or ice cold inside when people talk about how wonderful families are, how the holidays are all about family, or how sad the family are on a reality show when a member of the family has a serious problem. When *you* think of family, you are more likely to think of someone screaming in your face. If these Volcano people tended to be of one gender, you may have especially difficult issues with men or women, and as an adult believe on some level that *all* men or *all* women are cruel people.

The Iron Butterfly Syndrome

General Characteristics

An Iron Butterfly is a family member who insists that everything and everyone at all times should reflect *beauty*—no easy task in a love-less family. Consequently *beauty* is no longer something that exists in the eye of the beholder. Instead, for everyone, it is whatever the Iron Butterfly says it is—nothing more and nothing less. An Iron Butterfly's specific tastes may change, but the overarching tendency is for her to consider herself the foremost authority on what clothes should be worn, how a room should be appointed, what constitutes good music or literature, and—more importantly—what sorts of emotions and attitudes should be permitted within her domicile. If she finds any kind of anything to be unattractive or negative, it shall have no place in her world.

In fact, he may complain repeatedly that thanks to that unhappy story you told him, his entire day is *ruined.* If you hadn't bought that candy bar into the house with all those chemicals then his stomach would not now be hurting. That he took a bite himself is not the issue—*you* did it to him. You always bring ugliness with you.

To simplify, an Iron Butterfly will rapturously arrange followers in a vase, luxuriating in their beauty and fragrance as she liltingly hums away. Then you walk in the door, and she says—or screams—something hurtful at you. Then she returns to her flowers as though nothing has happened, merrily humming away. In other words, an *Iron* Butterfly. The world is made of love and beauty, damn it. She yells at you with an ugly, contorted face, then the phone rings, and she liltingly answers it, with a beatific smile on her face. Again, the message is all is lovely in her world except for you.

Yet, awful as you are in the Iron Butterfly's eyes, you must keep it all to yourself—or get better somehow, it's really none of his business how you do it. If you are in any way critical, sarcastic, or pessimistic, expect a lecture or sharp words about what an awful presence you are, how you're always trying to bring people down. She makes note of songs or stories with a single negative word in them—not a swear word, necessarily, but a word such as scared, sad, murder, or noisy. Everything must be a sign of love and beauty at all times.

Since society still often thinks that beauty is a woman's domain, not surprisingly, many Iron Butterflies are women.[1] She may or may not consider herself in sympathy with feminism and gender equality, but either way, she probably has not abandoned the more traditional roles and responsibilities assigned to women. If she works in an office, she may be a backstabber or prone to nasty fits of temper—so much so that others learn to stay away from her. Yet she will insist that she is a wonderful person who only likes nice things and she will be the first to suggest that everyone buy a gift for someone.

But Iron Butterflies can also be men, whether straight, bi, gay, or, for all intents and purposes, neuter. If he's straight, people probably have wondered if he isn't. Bisexuality here is often expressed through marriage to a woman—which happened for the sake of family tradition or religious values—and he sees men on the side. Yet he may be happy with this arrangement—even if others in his life are not—because he appreciates the aesthetic of being married to a woman, wearing a wedding ring, and being able to say, "My wife." But regardless of his sexual lifestyle, he can be as strict as a woman when it comes to a glass without a coaster under it, or as snobbish when it comes to having to deal with people who are beneath him—that is, family members.

In point of truth, the Iron Butterfly actually may walk a thin line where mental stability is concerned, but she does not see it that way. As far as she's concerned, the problem is everyone else. Yet beneath her fancy airs, she was probably deeply hurt for being in a loveless family. Maybe she really does have a strong aesthetic sense, and was made fun of because of it. And this strong aesthetic sense might have made all yelling and screaming—or the Zombie-like lethargy—seem that much worse.

In any case, over the years, being an Iron Butterfly has become a wall for her to hide behind—and to shift the blame. If it weren't for your utter lack of appreciation for beauty, or your bad vibes, or whatever is supposedly the matter with you, she'd have the beautiful world she deserves. It doesn't matter if the things she claims to appreciate are genuinely appreciated or not. She is trying to hide her true feelings. She is trying to say, "I am not like you other people." Though she claims to love harmony and balance, these apparently are the most fragile qualities, because a single crude remark causes them to vanish.

Not that he is always the living embodiment of gracious living. He can curse up a blue streak, yell, smash things, and even hit people. Yet once again, this somehow does not really happen in his mind.

Some Iron Butterflies do get out there and make something of themselves. In fact, the Iron Butterfly's intense desire to escape her loveless family helps motivate her, and she becomes successful in her chosen field.[2] If his work does not directly involve creativity, then perhaps he travels extensively, always has season tickets to the local symphony, or is a shrewd collector of art. Yet, even if she never leaves home or is poor as a church mouse, an Iron Butterfly still gives the impression of knowing about the finer things in life. Even if she cannot afford it, she probably will purchase at least one object that is monetarily way beyond her means, and feature it prominently in her home. If he lives in a low-income neighborhood, he can barely stand to give his neighbors the time of day.

When she has children, she is intensely particular about whom they may play with. Her standards for what constitutes an acceptable childhood companion can involve obvious things like social class or yes, ethnicity.[3] But it also may be that she thinks So-and-So dresses her children with good taste or has an elegant living room, so you therefore should be friends with this person's children. (This dictum was handed down to me, though I did not follow it, and by age 10 was getting into trouble for misbehaving with the *wrong* kids, some of whom I know to this day.) In fact, something about her planning her children's lives is quite similar to her, say, picking out the fabric for new drapes. Yet even if she was born, lived, and died in a ghetto, she always tried to make it clear to all within earshot that she was different from everyone else, and that her children were better than other people's children.

Flipping the coin over, not all wealthy people are Iron Butterflies. Many are capable of genuine friendship and know how to give and receive love. Also, since wealthy people often feel that they do not have to prove anything to anyone, they can be in some ways less concerned with whether they impress people, or not. It would be unrealistic to ask someone born into wealth to give away all of his money. Yet there are people who consider their material fortune to have both advantages and disadvantages. Some wealthy people may feel it keeps other people from getting to know them for who they are and sometimes they worry that people only associate with them for their money. Yet it would be naïve to think that wealthy people never match the description of an Iron Butterfly, and, in fact, many nonwealthy people read magazines or watch TV shows about the rich so that they may copy them.

But whether rich or poor, the Iron Butterfly can go on for hours about a meal in a restaurant, what someone was wearing, how a piece of music affected him, the flowers in a shop window, a picture in a magazine—anything that affirms his unmatched appreciation for all that is lovely in life. He talks about these things with the breathless enthusiasm that other people might reserve for talking about people whom they love.

There is something bordering on the fascist beneath the beatific smile and graceful manner of the Iron Butterfly. It isn't just that her tastes are so pronounced, but her absolute disdain for all that is beneath her—and a great deal is. While other people merely dislike a song, it gives the Iron Butterfly a *headache*. She might literally be frightened of a painting or piece of music that is anything less than tranquil. It is *evil*.

In fact, if he is spiritual, he probably is drawn only to what might be termed the nice stuff: God is love, God loves everyone, people are vessels of God's love, God lives in each of us so we are all divine creatures, love conquers evil and hate, and so on.[4] There is no room at all for the more difficult challenges someone truly dedicated to the spirit might undergo, especially in today's challenging world. Dwelling on all that is considered as too negative by the Iron Butterfly. Indeed, if one is so negative as to threaten the aura of beauty she has endowed upon the world, she may yell and scream, or hit you, or break something over your head.

If she writes a letter or posts a web page, she probably goes on about how the birds are chirping, and the water in the pond is tranquil, and the flowers are all in bloom....I hope you get the idea. While many people appreciate the beauty of nature, for the Iron Butterfly it is something more—the manifestation of what she thinks is her inner existence. It's as if the birds came into existence to beautify her back yard. She neglects to mention that she stayed awake for two nights tending to Junior's chicken pox. Or if it is mentioned, it is in terms of what a beautiful experience it was to soothe her son, and how at the crack of dawn she saw the sunrise—again, nothing but upbeat stuff.

If he lives in a city, the Iron Butterfly concentrates on how culturally enriching it is, that just the other night he saw some opera, or ballet, or—to show how cool he is—he heard these great street musicians, or saw a beautiful mural on the wall of a building in an Hispanic neighborhood. In fact, he becomes quite chauvinistic about the city he lives in, insisting that New York, or Pittsburgh, or Boise is *the* only place anyone could *possibly* want to live.

If she possesses some measure of talent, it is used exclusively within the narrow confines of what she considers beautiful. He renders an oil painting of, say, a vase of roses, or a bough of cherry blossom in his window. She writes a poem or song about the glories of spring. Other sorts of things—even mundane things—are too depressing, and if you say something like, "There was a pile of puke on the sidewalk next to a homeless man," he will criticize you for always dwelling upon the negative. If you mentioned that you called 911 because the person seemed to need help, the Iron Butterfly might lecture you on how, while that was okay, the real truth of life comes from meditation, or from being at one with nature. For all her talk about happiness, it takes next to nothing to make her feel bad.

Though constantly enraptured by the wonder and awe all about her, the Iron Butterfly has trouble with humor. For humor is somehow too human an experience for her. It is crude and takes away from the sublime seriousness of beauty. If he does laugh, it is usually over something he himself has just said, or in any case probably something no one else thinks is funny. She is seldom if ever the life of the party. Like someone who's never heard rock music before trying to move to the beat, she has little sense of how to deliver a joke, and probably seldom—or perhaps never—does.

Probably he has no appreciation for your own tastes, and he—and his sympathetic wife—may criticize you severely for daring to play music that you like. It made his refined musical ear wince—it *hurt* him to have to listen. It's common for parents not to like the same music as their children, but with the Iron Butterfly this matter becomes something much more profound. Why should The Great He have to listen to something so beneath his highly refined tastes. Every second he listens, it's as if another piece of his soul dies.

Many kinds of people overspend, especially in today's world. But the Iron Butterfly may consider herself especially entitled to spend too much money. It is never a happy occasion when there are more bills than there is money to pay them. But in a loveless family such a situation only becomes that much more exacerbated. However, the Iron Butterfly may still cling to the notion that this is not her fault. She *needs* these things and everyone else is just too insensitive to understand this.

When it comes to taking sides in a loveless family, it is less to do with the issue at hand than it does with who is on which side already. Whoever has the most talent, or pseudo talent, or class, or pseudo class gets his loyalty. An Iron Butterfly may say of a particularly difficult person, "You have to understand, she wanted to be a ballet dancer." If an Iron Butterfly met a serial killer, she may decide he's actually a good person, because he has a talent for drawing, or enjoys classical music.

The Iron Butterfly's snobbery also may, of course, include prejudice against various kinds of people. She may *hate* music, food, or customs from a culture that she considers to be low class. In fact, she may hate it without knowing anything about it. One Iron Butterfly of my acquaintance once heard a song sung by Ella Fitzgerald and said, "Oh my God, she doesn't sound black." It was hard to decide what to respond to first—that this 40-something-year-old, urban man who considered himself highly cultured had never even heard Ella Fitzgerald before, or his approbation and surprise that she didn't sound black. The prejudice here was both racist and classist—black music represented low music that did not evoke the pleasant, high-style living that Ms. Fitzgerald's rich and melodic voice embodied. So what sort of fluke of the universe was this? In the end, I decided not to even bother responding.

Yet there is an up side to growing up with an Iron Butterfly. Though their tastes are often pretentious, based on making an impression rather than on actual enjoyment, it may have been good for some of this to rub off on you. In a household devoid of art, it may have been good for you to learn of the existence of Picasso, Cezanne, and Van Gogh. The same can hold true of music, literature, or things like how to dress, or how to decorate a room. The actual tastes of the Iron Butterfly may have been shoddy—but at least this person got you thinking outside the box. You were exposed to a sense that there was more to life than what transpired within the walls of the family home. And acting superior to other family members, though ludicrous in many ways, is at least one way of mentally or physically distancing yourself from an unloving environment.

The Effects of Growing Up with an Iron Butterfly

The Iron Butterfly is not an easy person to like over time. One must be quite naïve or pretentious to enjoy her company for long. Further, since any advice or help he gives you is either based on highly superficial standards, or is intentionally aimed at not helping you so that he can still seem superior, you are unlikely to want to be around him unless you are extremely desperate. Indeed, as she grows older and it becomes more apparent that the bubble she lives in burst many years ago, she may become increasingly mentally unstable, or turn to drugs or alcohol to lessen her unhappiness. So all things considered, this is not someone you probably want in your life beyond an occasional short visit. Indeed, you may enjoy poking holes in his everything-is-beautiful universe by never speaking to him again. After all, how beautiful is that?

However, this does not mean she had no effect on you. Particularly if you were singled out by an Iron Butterfly as someone with potential—which is to say someone who could become like her—you may find it difficult to shake off all of her highly dogmatic opinions, beliefs, and tastes. You may hate this person, yet be all but foaming at the mouth when someone offers a contrary point of view.

Also, unless life forced you to come down from your high horse, you indeed may be something of a snob yourself at times, and consider many people beneath you. Nobody much likes a loser—that's why they're *called* losers—but for you, there is the additional burden of someone of your caliber having to deal with such a person. Every additional word in a brief conversation might as well be a dagger through your heart.

Even if you keep it mostly to yourself, you probably are very critical of other people. This does not just mean that you are critical of people who are greedy, or dishonest, or unkind. But when people do not dress well in your opinion, or lack what you consider good manners, you may just shut them out of your life. Someone who, for example, does not send you a thank you note (or email) for a gift you gave him is certainly not worth knowing as far as you are concerned.

This does not mean you act exactly like the Iron Butterfly in your life. In many ways, you may make a point of doing the opposite. You may have terrible table manners, or swear every other word, or dress like a slob. Yet, at the same time, you still know what is supposedly proper and may give yourself certain latitudes that you may not give to others.

It's not unlikely that you are bad with money. Even if you have little to show for it, you probably tend to overspend, because your early years did nothing to teach you something so basic as whether you were rich or poor. Plainly stated, you were not taught the value of a dollar. If, as a teenager, you asked permission to get an after-school job, you may have been told no, because others would then assume you came from a poor family.

Since you alternately felt better off and worse off than other kids, you also have issues with feeling a shared group identity. If people are nice to you, you may welcome their attention at first, but at some point you start to shy away. That these people are not the superior beings you thought they were at first may well play into your decision to back off. Small groups that you either lead or are active in often become smaller over time. This could be for any number of reasons, but it could also be that you are the opposite of a social magnate.

Certainly you stand out in a crowd, and on the surface of things you may be perfectly polite, but you do not give people enough of yourself for them to feel a real connection. You may be the kind of person who leads conversations, and raises interesting topics, and maybe even makes people laugh—but then you do not get invited to the party.

If you are poor, you may have difficulty getting anyone to help you, because superficially you seem intelligent, well informed, and capable. It is difficult for people to believe that you can barely pay the rent, because surely there is something more you could be doing for yourself. If money is not a problem, you may still have a tendency to make acquaintances more than actual friends. And so when faced with a problem or tragedy that transcends how much money you have in the bank, you still may not have many people you can turn to for genuine support.

You may share the repugnance of the Iron Butterfly(s) in your past for anything negative or disturbing. But you also may go out of your way to seek out *only* that which is negative and disturbing, which—as much as you hate to admit it—does depress and debilitate you over time. Essentially, you live an ongoing inner battle as to whether the human experience is good or bad, happy or depressing. However, with maturity and professional guidance, you may learn to find a happy balance.

12

The Interloper Syndrome

General Characteristics

Loveless families often also try to keep what the family is really like a secret.[1] This can be out of shame, narcissism, fear of legal authority, or simple social insecurity. Barely able to cope with each other, loveless family members may experience anxiety when trying to connect to outsiders. Even when someone likes to give parties—as someone in my family did—they were for a special crowd of people only. And these child-alienating events with drunken old men in the living room and their drunken wives in the kitchen—parties that children nonetheless were forced to attend—did not reflect everyday family life. Still, despite the best efforts of all involved, there can be spillage.[2] On several occasions in my own childhood, a teacher, principal, or guidance counselor tried to do a sort of intervention—before the term was in common usage—by suggesting to my elders that possibly I was not the world's happiest or most well-adjusted child. (When anyone asked directly how I was, or how my home life was, I always said everything was fine.) Needless to say, these efforts resulted in nothing but my being made to feel guilty for making extra work for the family.

In any event, outsiders often see things plainly enough, and some of them may try to force themselves on the family in order to make it better. The school officials I just mentioned in my own case stayed within the boundaries of their profession. They tried, they failed, they moved on. But there can be other people who want to stage a kind of hostile takeover of the family. And bad as the family already is, the presence of these people usually proves highly disruptive over time, and drives even more wedges between family members.[3]

In the context of the loveless family, an Interloper may be someone completely unrelated, or it may be someone who is now related through marriage, such as a stepparent.

There are successful stepfamilies and blended families who are willing to do the work it takes to create a reconfigured loving family. This hard work includes a willingness to listen, to be honest, and to be patient—in so many words, a willingness to love. But in other instances, a stepparent is insecure when children do not instantly regard him or her as a new mother or father.[4] Further, legally the stepparent may have no authority over the children. If the stepparent herself grew up without good examples to learn from, she falls back on what she knows—trying to control everyone—as a means of warding off this insecurity.

The original blood parent may reach a point in which she has to decide between her new spouse and her children. Even when she chooses her children and separates from the heretofore stepfather, there will still be serious adjustments that the children have to make. If their father or mother remarries or re-cohabitates time and time again, the children may grow to see their parents as something less than positive role models. Especially if the parents appear to have little regard for how the changes are affecting their children's lives, the children's resentment may fester into estrangement over time.

When someone is unable to raise his or her children for whatever reason, a blood relative may step in to gain custody of the young people, or have a kind of informal custodial arrangement. Sometimes the actual parent truly should not be raising children: he has a serious drug problem, she is incarcerated, he is physically abusive, she simply abandoned her family, and so forth. When parents die or are murdered, other relatives may generously open their hearts and homes to the children left behind.

When there was more stigma against unwed motherhood, sometimes the child was taught that her grandmother was her mother, and her actual mother her older sister. But it is also possible that long-standing rivalries are involved. A woman's mother or sister may seek to humiliate her by showing what a better job they can do of raising her children than she can. Or they may use the child to take out their resentments on.

But whether a relative or not, the Interloper is someone who, in so many words, cannot mind his own business. Most everyone gossips sometimes, but some people are raised in such a way as to conclude that gossip is the only means to connect to other people. And gossip, of course, is made all the more juicy when it is negative.[5] "Mary and Joe are happy" simply is not as interesting, and does not lend itself to elaboration, as much as saying, "Mary and Joe are miserable." So to feel connected to others, the Interloper must engage in gossip and intrigue. She tells this to this person, tells some other person not to talk to you, still yet another person about this, and so on. And since loveless families are likely to feature a great deal of unhappiness, the Interloper may feel she has struck a virtual gold mine.

Another reason for becoming an Interloper is that, if someone is busy with everyone else's problems, he doesn't have to look at his own life. He may even appear to be someone who is extremely wise and happy by comparison. So he may even convince himself that he has no problems.

Also, she may have few close friends or family members herself. So he is like a bossy stray cat that insists a family adopt him. The problem usually is not shyness on her part. She may well be an extremely charismatic person who stands out in a crowd. "Other people can only give you a little," she seems to say, "while I can give you so much more." There may be an appealing unconventionality about her, which she uses to get noticed. Or, flipping the coin over, if a family already is rather unconventional, she determines to bring conformity and order to it. Principles—or at least fake principles—matter more to her than other people's feelings. She thinks nothing of telling someone off or being insulting. Yet she is far from indifferent as to how other people regard her. While being off-putting is second nature to her, somehow everyone should always welcome her presence just the same.

When he is a nonrelative, he probably ingratiates himself extremely quickly on one or more family members. He may have quite a lot in common with a family member: a similar background, interest, or pretentiousness. Soon the children are to think of him as an uncle. He may start calling the grandmother of the family *mom*. Whether or not he literally seeks to replace one of the family members—such as marry one of the parents—for all intents and purposes he seeks to be your *real* father or brother in spirit.

At first, you a may find this extremely seductive. Though you often feel that most people couldn't care less about you, here is this interesting and lively person who has singled you out as someone special. To use a well-worn phrase, you seem as if you've always known each other. Or that is, if you are the primary individual being sought out. Others in the family may be relegated to much less important roles.

If the Interloper is a new stepparent (or even cousin-in-law) she may also strive to make a strong impression at first. But since she is supposed to become an actual family member, especially if she is a stepparent, the initial encounters may not go as smoothly as they would if she were simply a hanger-on. Any family may have questions about just who this new family member is. But in loveless families, people may be especially wary of newcomers, or lack the social skills to be truly welcoming. Even if the introductions occur over a perfectly pleasant meal, the following day or week suspicions, criticisms, or just a general sense of distance comes into play.

Either way, the Interloper has big plans for the family. Whether the Interloper puts up a nice façade to win you over, or—as stepparents sometimes do—protests a bit too much that he is, in fact, a parental figure in your life, you can almost see the gears in his mind turning. Even if he has a gregarious personality, there is something about him that seems odd or untrustworthy. What your instincts are telling you is that this person is disingenuous.

The Interloper may know exactly what she wants: maybe she wants the family jewels, or to have her friend's partner all to herself. In other instances, the Interloper only knows she wants escape from the reality of her life—be it loneliness, a bad marriage, or whatever—and that this new family presents her with a detour.

He may come across as someone who has everything the family needs or as someone for whom the family has something *he* needs. If a stepmother says, "I've always wanted children and now I have five all at once," she may truly mean it and be happy. But if she has Interloper tendencies, she may actually be thinking about how to get the kids out of the house, or of all the new rules she'll be imposing, because she actually has little feeling for children. She may especially go out of her way to do things differently than the previous parent did. If dinner has always been at 6, she will move to 6:30. Things that children heretofore did not have to ask permission for now require permission. A nonrelative may interfere with the parent's plans or policies. If children are being abused or neglected, by all means contact authorities at once. But if, for example, a child is sent to her room for saying something inappropriate, the Interloper will go to her room and go to the parent to try to make a different arrangement that is really none of his business.

Childhood friendships usually are relatively informal. When not in school children may play with their friends most all the time, and depending on where you live, they may come over without being invited. As we get older and more settled, we tend to see friends less often, and many adults would not think of barging over to someone's home unasked. But the Interloper knows no such boundaries. He invites himself over all the time. He offers to cook dinner for the family. He invites the kids to go to the circus with him. And these offers tend to be made without checking with the adults first, which puts them in an awkward position. Or, if he is a stepfather, he may automatically plow his way in to everyone's life, without regard for the notion that relationships need time to grow. His message is: "You can tell me anything, you should come to me with everything, I can do more for you than anyone else."

The thing about the Interloper is that whether it's through marriage or friendship, she essentially has, at most, only a couple of ties to family members. But the entire brood is expected to go along for the ride, whether they like it or not—or whether they like *her* or not. So once again, despite the superficial claim of being helpful or wanting to know you, you are not being treated as a human being with a right to your own feelings and opinions.

When an Interloper senses that his days are numbered in the family, he probably will try to get people on his side. Since the family is a mess anyway, it may be fairly easy to convince one or more well-placed players that the Interloper is right about whatever it is, and the family is wrong. Thus, even when the Interloper claimed to be trying to help the family, his lasting contribution may be even greater emotional distance between family members. Interlopers are not beyond twisting things around or lying outright about what somebody did or said.

Interlopers also have a way of not delivering what they promise. Stepparents who promise all sorts of fun times ahead instead become cold, impatient, and dictatorial. Other Interlopers may forget about those circus tickets after all, or show up five hours late on the evening he said he'd cook dinner. He also is not the good listener or wise guru that he promised to be, and he may make you feel worse than before you confided in him. (Any or all of this could be because, unbeknownst to you, the Interloper has mental issues or substance-abuse problems.)

Interlopers often have a short lifespan within the family. Bad marriages end or nonrelatives are chased away. But sometimes they hang on for decades, even if only through one or two family members, and possibly in secret. If the marriage does not end, the Interloper may have been successful in driving a wedge between you and the relative he married. And if you have never been the primary object of the Interloper's affection, you probably could disappear from her life and she would barely notice.

One positive thing about Interlopers is that, at least for a short while, they promise change—and if your loveless family is utterly lackluster, an injection of new activity may seem like a waterhole in a desert. Some of their nosiness and desire to control may produce ideas or developments that prove useful. And if you already do not get along with your family, the stepparent who tries to alienate you ironically may be doing you a favor of sorts. You may find you do better in life with fewer family ties, however sad that reality may be. Also, if you are not unwittingly placed in the middle of an Interloper's battles with the family, you can learn from a negative example what kind of family life—if any—you want for yourself. You may find comfort in the notion that whatever your problems are you are not as messed up as these other people. You may even reach the point where you look back on the Interloper's trouble-making with a wry amusement. Finally, since even stepparents are not blood relatives, an Interloper may provide you with a cathartic opportunity for self-determination. It is easier to tell and Interloper, "Stop telling me what to do," or "I know more about me than you do, so shut up," than to tell your intimidating mother or father.

The Effects of Growing Up with an Interloper

Depending on the depth and duration of your association with an Interloper, you may have a confused sense of even who your family *is*. Even if it has been decades since you've had contact with this person— even if the person is no longer living—he probably looms large in your imagination. Since you already do not feel close to family members, the Interloper may have had a long-term effect of making you feel even less close. Since even who your family is a complicated question, this may well add to your sense of confusion about life, and how nothing can ever be as simple for you as it is for other people. When there is a dispute over family history, you may be all the more unsure as to which side of the story to believe—if either. You may wonder if anyone ever tells the truth or is worthy of your trust.

Since Interlopers actually are trying to self-promote more than help others, they may have had the effect of depleting your already weak self-image. Any of your own ideas you have shared about yourself were probably dismissed as wrong, which confounded your ability to trust your own judgments. You may also feel very easily misunderstood. To guard against this, you may go out of your way to preface your comments or explain them in great detail, to insure you are not misunderstood. While many students try to keep a paper assignment as short as possible, you may have the opposite problem of keeping it within the assigned page limits. You want to make sure you've been clear and haven't left anything out.

Most everyone sometimes plans in advance what they are going to say to someone. Job interviews, asking the boss for a raise, asking someone to marry you—there are many moments in life in which we may write down what we're going to say in advance, or go over it in our minds many times over. But you may have a tendency to do this about most anything—even when nothing much is at stake. You may also try to plan in advance things the other person will want to hear in order to get them on your side, so that certain topics or criticisms against you do not come up.

You may also be confused about how to regard the Interloper over time. They have a funny way of getting under your skin. So even if she was mean to you, or you can see now that he was crazy, the very fact of their presence in your life may seem too puzzling to comprehend. In a negative way, blood can be thicker than water, so things that were already wrong with your family may instead now seem like the Interloper's fault. The Interloper did indeed take advantage of a situation for personal gain. But the groundwork for family misunderstandings was probably already in place. In fact, you might feel sorry for the Interloper, and without professional help you may tend to look back and think it was all your fault, when it wasn't.

PART THREE

PHYSICAL AND MENTAL CONDITIONS, AND DEATH

Even the strongest of families is challenged when one or more family members face a serious condition.

13

Dealing with Serious Physical Conditions

Obviously, even the closest and most loving of families is challenged when one or more family members develop or are born with a serious physical condition. This can mean an illness or injury that requires special attention and/or may lead to death, or a physical challenge that creates special needs. Indeed, a once-close family may emerge less close based on how they deal with these situations. Strong love may turn into weakened love as the family grapples with how to make sure everyone's needs are met. On the other hand, strong love may remain strong or become even stronger. People may even sincerely say they feel blessed by the challenge. This does not mean they respond perfectly, because there is no perfection where human nature is concerned. Of course mistakes will be made. There will be good days and bad days. There will be arguments, and moments of frustration, and moments of profoundest sorrow. But out of it all, a team spirit prevails. And so there also will be moments of joy, triumph, and humor. Why? Because the players involved really do care. Someone being hearing or vision impaired, or wheelchair mobile, is simply a normal part of family life.

But in loveless families, illness or serious physical conditions are just another nuisance in a long line of nuisances. When people don't really love someone much—or not at all—but are *supposed* to act like they do, they may secretly resent the family member for having cancer or being unable to walk. And to some extent, their resentment is justified, since they do not really regard the sick person as a human being. So not only will this nonentity be taking up the family members' time, but she will be distorting their emotional worlds. Family members will have to pretend to have a level of concern that they do not really have. And pretending to emotions one does not possess can be nearly as exhaust-ing as having to attend to another's special physical needs.[1] In fact, the latter might become an accepted part of one's daily routine, while the former will cause resentments to build.

In loveless families, even a child getting the flu can be perceived as nothing but a nuisance. The reaction the parent gives the child is not so much, "I hope you feel better," as it is, "God damn it, what now?" The parent(s) may not believe the child is sick and that the child is just faking it to miss school. This obviously has been known to happen. But sometimes, even after it's shown that the child has a fever, the parent may senselessly maintain that the child is faking, or did it on purpose. Perhaps the parent cares only about the child being a straight-A student, as if the child were a straight-A machine. And so the parents are angry that the child is spoiling her chances for the future they have planned for her—without asking the child if this is the future she wants. Or maybe the parent only cares about work, and resents having to miss a few hours or a few days to tend to the sick child. Some parents may also take even a single sneeze as a sign that other people will think they are bad parents and that the child is just trying to make them look bad. Or perhaps the parents despise weakness, and think the child is being weak—especially if the parents see the child as an it or a thing that exists to be their personal psychological experiment.

If the child is seriously ill or injured, obviously parents are supposed to act concerned, so they may put on one face to the doctors or con-cerned neighbors, and another face to the child himself. The parents may call the child stupid or clumsy, or a pain in the ass. Or maybe the parent's silence says it all. On the surface of things, the parents may clean up the mess on the bed or reconnect the catheter, but they do not demonstrate interest in how the child feels.

A parent might also insist that the child grows up, or acts like a man as he experiences pain, or undergoes procedures the adult himself never had to face. Yes, it is true that many forms of illness or physical limitation benefit from one's learning self-reliance. A lifetime spent in self-pity is not likely to be a lifetime that accomplishes much. Normal routines—which include discipline and boundaries—may be impor-tant in helping the child feel like a normal person and a regular part of the family. But encouraging a child to develop inner strength or a can-do attitude will not be effective if it is not backed up by love. Instead, a parent will seem like a ruthless drill sergeant or sadistic gym teacher. The child feels inadequate and a nuisance to all concerned.

If there are other, non-afflicted children in a loveless family, a great many sibling-rivalry games may turn into lifelong battles.[2] Perhaps the parents simply assume that the other children understand that their needs do not matter as much as those of the sick child. The other children may be labeled good or bad on the basis of how little attention they require. Also, which child helps out the most may determine the pecking order among siblings. However, sometimes helping out is like being in the hot seat. You may not be thanked at all, and instead criticized for not doing everything to perfection, or making other people in the family look bad.

There are few, if any, discussions, embraces, or opportunities to express how anyone feels. This can lead to all sorts of animosity: hatred toward the parents; hatred or jealousy toward the sick child; or trying or getting in trouble to get attention. The children may also grow up believing that they should never have any needs and never cause anyone the slightest inconvenience—or, they were raised that way but know it was wrong, so they act out against this limitation. Indeed, it is possible for a child to help out a great deal *and* be rebellious at the same time. Neither role seems to bring positive attention into the child's life.

Obviously, it is challenging for any parent to find the right balance if someone has, say, four children and one of them is terminally ill, born physically different, or suffers serious permanent damage from a car accident. But in loving families, people *try* to figure it all out—and even consult professionals—while in loveless families, all the imbalance and ill will just sort of flails about, stuffed one moment, exploding into rage the next.

Parents themselves may undergo tension in their intimate relationship when faced with a child in physical crisis or with special needs. But when love is being trampled on, little is done to explain what is going on to the children—or maybe either or both parents try to win the children to their side, as often happens in ugly divorces. Or maybe the parents disagree over which child is being good or bad, or needs more attention. Factions are formed, as if being a member of the family is a form of warfare or competition.

Another possibility is to deny that much of anything is wrong.[3] The child *will* of course get better, or the situation is no big deal, so no discussion is needed at all. Denial can spring from love—from a fear or dread about what this child you love so much may be going through. But on the other hand, denial also can spring from a place of non-love. It simply is too much bother to dwell on the realities of the situation and consider that there are challenges to face. Perhaps the child is even sent away to live elsewhere, because a parent does not want to stop partying, working, or drinking a lot. If the child is still around, she may be told something hollow like, "Stop having a chip on your shoulder," or, "You're lucky to be alive at all."

Loveless indifference can sometimes pass for love in these situations. A parent, who in truth can't be bothered with wanting his child to accomplish all she can, may come across to others as pampering or spoiling his daughter by letting her develop bad habits for her physical pain or limitations. This also happens between spouses. A loving family can watch helplessly as (for example) their severely injured child becomes addicted to pain killers and they do not know what to do about it. But in a loveless family, no one can be bothered much.

Similar patterns may occur if it is a parental or adult figure who is seriously ill, or injured, or has special needs. There may be denial that anything is wrong and children may even be yelled at if they ask, "Is daddy going to die?" Father himself, in his ill state, may behave in ways he normally would not. Between coping with the reality of his own mortality, or with the side effects of medical treatment, he may become a difficult person to be around. But again, loveless families make no effort to help children through these trying times. The children, however young, simply are supposed to understand, and, in fact, may be scolded for even daring to suggest that they had their feelings hurt. And since loveless families may not even discuss what is wrong with the person in the first place, the child is left feeling confused and alone. If the adult obviously is suffering or unhappy, and the child has no support system, the child may have little sense as to the meaning of life, or whether it even is worth living. Again, the child may learn to keep these questions a private mater, as obviously no one around her is interested in providing answers or even in listening.

Although there is little, if any, communication about what the actual situation is—as well as little, if any, comfort offered to the children—they are expected to know somehow what is happening and make it their main priority. Having fun with friends may be deemed inappropriate; the child is made to feel guilty for wanting to be like other kids. Also, if the problem is kept a secret from the outside world—which is likely to happen when the impression one makes on others outweighs seeking emotional support and honesty—children may feel that much more lost and confused. Everything is fine—no, wait a second, how can everything be fine if no one is supposed to know this thing that is happening?

(I could write an entire book on how *not* to handle family illness by writing about my mother's illness and death. But for the time being, I simply will mention that I was told repeatedly that if anyone asked how my bedridden mother was, I was to say she was fine. I did not know what was really wrong with her, and when I asked, I was yelled at for asking. I went to a religious school and every morning students offered prayers for specific people. After wrestling with my conscience for about a year, I finally told the class that my mother was sick. The teacher asked what she was sick with and I said I didn't know. She asked how long my mother had been sick and I said, "About a year." The teacher then asked why I didn't say anything sooner about this. I said I didn't know.)

The Effects of Growing Up in a Household Where There Is a Serious Physical Condition

In a loveless family, the lethargy, rage, or lack of emotional support that accompanies the fact of someone having serious physical issues may render you someone who has extreme difficulty emotionally connecting to others.

Because you were not allowed to engage in a normal range of responses regarding the sick or physically challenged person in your past, you may be uncertain as to what you actually do feel. At times it may seem as though you simply do not feel the same things other people feel. Perhaps you have even been criticized by others for not being in touch with your feelings, or maybe even not feeling anything at all. Yet at other moments you may decide your real problem is that you feel things too deeply, much more than anyone could ever understand or appreciate.

However, since these deep feelings are a source of pain, as you get older you may decide that an unfeeling persona is much more convenient. Better that people think you are emotionally disconnected than to have to go to that place of confusion and unhappiness. You may identify with songs or characters in movies that express an absence of feeling, and decide it is sexy or interesting to be this way.

Actually, you have good reasons for keeping things to yourself. Whenever you tried to do otherwise, it ended badly. And even today, even when people actually do care about you, they may go about it in an awkward or inappropriate way. Yelling at someone to open up is only going to make them shut down. And you may feel some genuine resentment when people try to pry too deeply. They did not go through what you went through and might well be just as closed-mouthed if they had. If someone says something like, "I had a terrible childhood—my father hardly ever went to my soccer games," you may resent it, given what you had to go through by comparison. When people actually *do* suffer, they often *don't* want to talk about it.

If you do take the risk of sharing with people, what you have to say may prove too much for the listener, so she says little in response, if anything. You may try this person or that group to talk about what you went through, but if nobody much seems to care, you stop trying.

Another trap that you may have experienced occurs when people *do* respond to what you have to say. Indeed, it is the only thing they want to talk about, and so again you relive feeling like an it or a thing. A theoretical concept that someone or some group wants to fix. There are people out there who can do both—treat you like an equal person in the moment and express sympathy for your past. But you may have to look carefully for them, and try not to be too disappointed when people—maybe even most people—are unable to do this.

You learned at a young age how to hide and control what you were really feeling, so it is not unlikely that as an adult you are, if anything, better at doing this. This may make for a rather skewed impression on others. However good you may think you are at hiding your feelings, they may spill out anyway, and in inappropriate ways. So you may seem like someone who pretends to be affable, but who does not pull it off. You go from calm, to rage, to calm again, with little in between.

On the other hand, maybe you do pull it off. Everyone thinks that you are this extremely thoughtful person whom nothing ever bothers. You start to feel the same way you felt growing up—like this thing that exists to make other people happy. So when you do reach a limit and express anger or hurt, they indeed abandon you, because you are not who you're *supposed* to be. The foundation that your friendship or relationship was built on was false, so it crumbles when the truth comes out. Underneath it all, you may develop into a cynical person who assumes people are just never going to understand you.

Also, you may feel a lack of sympathy or empathy for other people going through their own tribulations. If a middle-aged person tells you his father is sick, you may offer sympathy but on the inside feel: "So what? I had to go through that and worse when I was 5 or 12 and no one ever cared."

In sum, there are many situations that other people take for granted, but which, for you, are far more complicated and perturbing than you let on. If the afflicted family member in your past was unkind to you, you may well find it especially confusing to sort out how you feel. And since children model their behavior by the examples they were given, you may be treating other people in some of these same unkind ways, though it may be way too painful for you to come to terms with this.

14

Dealing with Serious Mental Conditions

Dealing with a family member who has mental issues can raise many of the same concerns as dealing with someone with physical issues. Indeed, making a distinction between the physical and the mental is sometimes a dubious endeavor. The medical knowledge base in some cultures makes far less of a distinction between the physical and the mental than ours does. There is evidence of physiological or genetic causes for some conditions that we view as mental. Eating disorders and addictions likewise blur the distinction between the mental and the physical. (So feel free to think of these conditions as either or both, as far as this book is concerned.) There also, of course, are children born with Down's syndrome, autism, or Williams syndrome (to name a few), in which again, both physical and mental issues become paramount. Brain injuries that cause a change in behavior or cognition of course also raise both physical and mental issues. There are also illnesses that compromise the body but not the mind, but other people may not understand (for example) that someone with cerebral palsy or multiple sclerosis still has her mind intact.

But a crucial difference between conditions *commonly* viewed as physical versus mental is that mental conditions are often less obvious or understood. If someone has a debilitating disease, was born without or lost a body part, or cannot walk, see, or hear, it is apparent. The physical dimension of the condition per se is difficult to dispute. Dealing with the situation is largely a matter of personal adjustment and training—along with technology, surgery, and/or medicine.

Yet, a mental condition may be harder for people to accept—including the self. People may die never knowing that they suffered from a psychotic or neurotic condition, and the families they leave behind may be mystified by what they had to deal with all those years. Even when someone is diagnosed, she—or other family members—may deny the diagnosis, or proclaim the condition has been cured when it has not.

Since conditions such as psychosis, chronic depression, obsessive compulsion, eating disorders, and addictions are viewed as mental in origin, there is a tendency for people to think these problems should simply be able to vanish.[1] The behavior of the afflicted individual does not make sense, so he should be able to just stop doing it—through willpower, by being yelled at, or by being logically told why what he is doing is wrong. Even close, loving families make these mistakes. But over time, at least some and maybe all family members listen and learn, because they truly do love and care about the person with problems.

However, in loveless families, in which people aren't treated as people, family members may stubbornly insist over time that there is no problem, that there used to be a problem but there isn't one now, or that the problematic individual just doesn't know how to follow good advice and has no willpower.[2] The denial is not coming from a place of love, so much as from an inability or refusal to honor someone's humanness. The ill person simply is a problem, an embarrassment, a bad reflection on the self, or on the family. In other words, an it, or a thing, or a concept instead of a person. If the person commits suicide or dies from an accidental overdose, family members still cannot be bothered much. They'll say something like, "She made her own bed so she had to sleep in it," or "He's been dead to me for many years anyway."

A variation on this theme again involves turning a person into an object, but the object is more like a doll or houseplant. One or more family members decide they can cure the sick person with vitamins, or vegan diets, or teaching them yoga, or getting them to read a book. But the do-gooder is likely to lose patience quickly when the homemade soup or walk in the park does not do what the do-gooder assumes it will do. The afflicted person may get blamed for simply being beyond help or for not taking seriously the advice being offered by the do-gooder. In a loveless family, people are not taught proper boundaries, so one family member may think another family member is her personal property, and when the other family member does not do whatever she wants, she cannot accept it. The failure of the effort may result in yelling and screaming, physical violence, or disavowing the self from the sick person.

I once heard of a mother whose daughter told her she was suicidal. The mother's response was to tell the daughter that if she attempted suicide the mother would call the police and have her put into the juvenile justice system for being incorrigible. The daughter attempted suicide. Sure enough, she was turned over to the police. To the best of my knowledge, professional therapy never came up as an option.

On the other hand, sometimes people get so little emotional support from anyone in the family that a mentally ill family member is the one individual that is available to the lonely person. (Perhaps other family members have distanced themselves from the ill individual.) This is likely to be a volatile relationship over time. It's unfair to expect someone who is mentally ill to hold all the answers to life or to never relapse into their illness, and the lonely person may be better off seeking professional guidance.

Mental issues also, of course, often result in a distorted perception of reality or outright lying. What seems obvious common sense to even a small child might get twisted all around by the adult with a mental condition. So not only are your emotional needs not met, but neither are your cognitive ones. The part of you that simply wants to make sense of the world and receive validation that you are capable of thinking clearly also suffers.

Especially when family ties are already weak, someone with serious mental issues may be quite skillful at stirring the proverbial pot. People who already have little feeling for each other may engage in hurtful arguments over the addict or person with bipolar disorder. The afflicted individual may have little ability or inclination to take responsibility for her own actions, and may even enjoy putting the blame on other people. After all, she doesn't really like these people much, and she might get some crumbs of attention or sympathy if people think that whatever happened wasn't her fault. Also, of course, if she's an addict or has a compulsive disorder she may see in this person she doesn't really care about an opportunity to get money in order to continue her destructive behavior.

Yet a mentally afflicted person can also feel all but invisible and be made to feel extremely guilty for being such a bother.[3] The family may also harbor superstitions about mental conditions—that only bad people are mentally ill, or unhappy, or become addicts. Perhaps a boy is extremely depressed, but has learned the hard way that it is useless to expect any viable support from his family. So as he gets older he cuts his family from his life, or blandly—and resentfully—says he is doing fine when forced to communicate with them.

As stated earlier, even close, loving families may have to deal with a family member who suffers from any number of mental conditions— even suicidal tendencies. But in such families there is a willingness to talk about it, and seek a viable solution if at all possible. A child can say, "Mom, I'm bulimic," or "Dad, I can't sleep without narcotics," or "Grandma, I think I'm going crazy." Even if the efforts to help fail, there was at least communication and moments of love, and concern.

But loveless families don't want to deal with any of this. A sister who gets drunk every day just needs to find a hobby. A child failing in school just needs to buckle down and concentrate. A teenager shooting heroin just needs to make nicer friends. If someone was traumatized for having been sexually molested, they should just get over it, because it does no good to blame your problems on other people. Or maybe the nuisance in question was just born bad, and has no business being part of the family, where rules and appearance matter more than people, and where inertia does not like being interrupted. It is especially easy to reach this conclusion with an adopted child, foster child, stepchild, or a child raised by relatives other than her parents.

If a sibling of yours was the troubled person, there once again may have been an extreme imbalance of who got attention from whom, who was the nuisance (you, or the person with the problem), who was supposed to make it all better, or who got in trouble for even saying there *was* a problem. A sibling bordering on estrangement may act rather like a parent about to get divorced, and try to win you over to his side, creating a divided sense of loyalties.

Should a parental figure have had serious mental issues, you may have felt extremely guilty when you were angry with them or when you wished they'd go away. If you tolerated a great deal of mental or physical abuse from the parent, in a loveless family you were probably never comforted for this, nor was it recognized that perhaps you were a brave or patient person.[4] Instead, any time you did anything that did not help or seemed to make something worse, you had to endure considerable criticism. Nothing you ever did was right or good enough. Instead, most everything you did was considered wrong. If you were the family scapegoat, you were blamed for causing the problem: she stuck her wrists through the windows because you talked too loud, or whatever the case may have been. Again, you were not recognized as an actual person. It was all about how your technical existence did or did not make hassles for other people.

The Effects of Growing Up in a Household Where There Is a Serious Mental Condition

If you yourself were the afflicted individual, and you grew up in a loveless family, it's unlikely that your problems were understood by family members. Instead, your problems probably were ignored, minimized, or were a source of conflict in which you were cast as the bad one for making so much trouble. It's entirely possible that your condition was made worse by the way you were treated. And probably no one has apologized over the years, or if they did, it was too little too late.

If a mentally afflicted adult caused you serious harm, you may have difficulty accepting that he couldn't help it, because no one has ever acknowledged the pain that you suffered. You may relive many unpleasant episodes as you get older, and your rage or frustration may not diminish unless you get professional help. Otherwise, you may take out your sense of loss on innocent people, or on yourself. As an adult, you are bigger and stronger and smarter than when you were eight years old, and so you may fantasize about punching your father back, or telling your mother what you really thought at the time. Your fantasies may even be more extreme than this. Again, you should talk to a professional, and do not, repeat not, cross the line from fantasy into reality.

Other situations that arise—someone you work with, something one of your kids does—may trigger the unhappiness you had to endure while growing up. People refuse to recognize that you are telling the truth or have offered a viable opinion. People may twist situations around to make them your fault, and never admit that they are wrong. You may feel angry or despondent that you have to experience this all over again. Haven't you already paid your dues? You may turn your co-workers into stand-ins for your family, and inappropriately try to work through what you weren't able to work through when you were a child. You may decide: "No one's ever going to yell at me again," or "Nobody's ever going to ignore my needs again." It's important to remember that professional settings are not personal ones, and that no one goes to work to help anyone else through their problems with the past—except doctors and therapists, that is.

Whether you stay stuck in the past and still act like a rebellious teen-ager when you're 45, or if you go out of your way to avoid anyone who seems to have any problems whatsoever, the pain you grew up with is never far away. The world does not seem a particularly safe place, and if you get through a day, week, month, or year without anything going seriously wrong, you almost can't believe it.

In truth, there are many troubled or insensitive people out there, and it is highly unlikely you will never encounter any of them. Try to remember that someone you only met a short time ago is not re-ally your alcoholic father or bipolar cousin. This does not mean that you should tolerate unacceptable behavior from other people. But they may not realize what effect their behavior is having on you unless you tell them—or decide to stop seeing them.

At times, you may resent that you are a strong person—a *survivor*, as it is often called. Because in order to feel good about yourself or proud of the obstacles you've overcome, you have to feel happy and connected to life. If you're depressed or secretly angry at the world, you may feel something like: "Big deal, I survived my crazy mother. I had no *choice*." In fact, you may be envious or resentful of people who grew up in happier, more loving families. In a heartbeat, you'd trade being a survivor for having had a happy childhood, with relatives you enjoy seeing and can turn to with trust.

You may try to self-medicate through alcohol or drugs, or by always working, or through sex, or any number of other pursuits. On the sur-face, you may be respected—let's say you're a CEO or movie star. But underneath it all, you actually feel an affinity with, say, a homeless alcoholic. In fact, you may live in fear that you'll end up that way your-self, because secretly you do not believe in your good fortune or that anyone likes you. You succeeded to make the pain go away, and if it hasn't, you don't feel as happy as you'd hoped, even if others look up to you.

15

Dealing with Death

Sooner or later every human being dies, yet death itself remains something of a taboo subject in our society.[1] Science continues to promise—and often delivers—treatments that will enable people to live longer. Those who can afford it get plastic surgery to look younger—which in some cases may mean looking farther away from death. The popular media is always saying things like, "40 is the new 30," or "60 is the new 50." When someone dies in her 70s, it no longer seems like she died at an especially old age. More and more people are living to be 100 or more.[2] Obviously there is nothing wrong with wanting to live a long, healthy, and active life. But in the final analysis, there is no cure for death—only postponement.

There is no perfect way of dealing with the death of someone you love. The loss of a child is especially heartrending, and there are perfectly normal, loving people who never fully recover from it. At the same time, losing a parent before reaching adulthood will inevitably alter your life in significant ways. Further, the way someone dies can add to the sense of loss. If your daughter was raped and murdered, or your five-year-old son died of cancer, your grief may be that much more of a burden to carry through life.

Not only do people miss the person who died, but they also miss the special close relationship they had with him.[3] In dealing with the death of a loved one, most anyone can be bent out of sorts, and say or do things they would not normally say or do. Sometimes, heretofore close families will even fall apart.

Still, increasingly in today's world, there is support and information available on coping with the death of a loved one. And as with other kinds of family crisis, it is possible to make the remaining time the dying person has left really count for something. Even if the death is unexpected, it is possible for the surviving family members to remain close or even to get closer. Sometimes a death brings feuding individuals back together. When people have been given love, they have love in their hearts, and this can help them to construct a positive, happy life despite the losses they have suffered.

However, loveless families don't know quite what to make of death. When you do not really care about someone, or maybe intensely dislike her, what are you *supposed* to feel when she dies? In one family, a teenage girl is killed in a car accident, and the family can barely even begin to cope with the devastation of the sudden loss. In another family, a teenage girl is likewise killed in a car accident, and the pervasive attitude is more like, "So what's next?" or "I knew this would happen to her, she never listened." It's part of a continuum of lousy things that happen where the family is concerned. Or maybe someone uses the event as an excuse to draw attention to himself—or to drink more, or to spend more time *away* from the family.

There may be excessive bitterness over division of the estate, a contest over who loved or hated the person the most, who was most abused by him, or who feels the most sense of loss. It can also be exploited as an opportunity to vent animosity by playing the Blame Game—"It's *your* fault he got a heart attack," or "You never loved her and you know it." Matters may escalate to the point of physical violence or to people never speaking to each other again. There may also be a fleeting moment of sentiment that draws people together for maybe a day or so before returning to the more usual general sense of estrangement.

The death itself may punctuate long-standing resentments within the family. Maybe the way the family member died seemed to involve negligence on the part of the dead person (who was a selfish or careless person), the parents (who should've paid better attention), the siblings (who were always mean to the person who died), or the children (who neglected their parents and did nothing to help, even if the children were very young at the time). Grandparents, aunts, uncles, and cousins may also figure into the scenario.

Though people are loathe to admit it, there may also be a certain envy for the dead person.[4] Not that any of the remaining family members necessarily are suicidal. But the dead, as the old saying goes, are commonly believed to rest in *peace.* If you believe in an afterlife of some form, then you might also believe that the dead person is now in a better place. In other words, the dead person may be getting at least some fuss made over him (while you never get any), while at the same time he doesn't have to deal with the awful family anymore. He has paid his dues. He got to miss the latest squabble that, ironically enough, erupted at his memorial service. (Again, if you *are* suicidal, contact a professional at once.)

At the same time, individually the people in a loveless family do not automatically lack any thoughtfulness or feeling whatsoever. So, as with the loss of anyone, members of a loveless family might contemplate their own mortality or regret that they never got closer to the person who died because so much was left unsaid. But these more profound feelings are likely to leave as quickly as they came. And before long everything is back to its normal, distant state.

People may also be criticized by family members for *how* they grieve: you cried too little. You cried too much. You were too serious. You weren't serious enough. You dressed too somberly. You dressed too brightly. You shouldn't have spoken at the memorial. You should've spoken at the memorial. You shouldn't have even shown up. It's unforgivable that you didn't show up. You shouldn't have said hello to So-and-So. You should've said hello to So-and-So. People in a loveless family can use these criticisms as emotional scapegoats for their own mixed-up feelings. Rather than look inside themselves, loveless family members make an unkind remark about how someone at the funeral is dressed, or how over-dramatic someone is being.

In particular, children may be told that what happened wasn't so bad, that the dead person would want them to be happy, to stop crying and sing along with the hymn, or whatever is being used to minimize the sense of loss. But then when the child *does* stop acting sad, she may be told that she isn't showing enough grief or respect for the deceased.

What all these reactions are about is the adults trying to make the process easier for themselves by not having to deal with those pesky unnecessities called children. There can also be little sense that maybe, just maybe the most profound loss out of the whole thing is experienced by the deceased person's children. People with little sense of love will tend to dwell only on themselves, and so the grief of a 40- year-old sibling of the deceased matters more than the grief of the deceased person's children. The 40-year-old sibling does little, if anything, to help the children with the grieving process.

Yes, even in loveless families, children can feel the loss of a parent most acutely. Sometimes children in highly abusive or neglectful homes say they would rather stay there than be put in an unfamiliar but safer home environment. So the death of even a very bad parent can be devastating. While some people disown themselves from abusive or neglectful parents as they get older, other people stay in touch and even learn to tolerate the thoughtlessness of the parent, because they'd rather have him in their lives than not.

If a parental figure dies, the child of a loveless family is given little license to mourn. After a day or two, it becomes a nuisance, and since the child is not really a person, the token gestures the adults make to *cure* the child of grief are simply supposed to work, period. In other words, the child is expected to cognitively and emotionally process something that the adults themselves are unable to process. It reflects badly on the adults when these efforts do not work, and so these people quickly lose patience with the child. (In my own case, an aunt believed that if I played outside all day throwing a rubber ball against a wall, I would no longer feel bad.)

Also, since there is not appropriate supervision of siblings or cousins, other children may take it upon themselves to cure the child of his grief, with even more unhappy results. An older cousin thought that if I became a better baseball player, I would be *normal* again. While trying to teach me how to throw and hit better—and he lacked the maturity to be a patient teacher—he relentlessly made fun of me for feeling sad that my mother had died. One time, he literally knocked me out with a hardball. And the adults did nothing to stop this. He was never punished or told to act differently.

I did, however, find helpful support and a sense of genuine concern from kind neighbors. Not just over losing my mother—which I actually didn't talk about much, as I didn't know how—but, in general, making me feel welcome in their homes and respecting me as a person, even though I was still a child. Not surprisingly, I was strongly discouraged from forming bonds with outsiders. The kind neighbors across the street or a block away were disparaged. I was also made to feel guilty for taking up these people's valuable time. (I recall these people fondly, and feel a pang of sadness for not being able to stay in touch, as fate moved me about to other households in other places.)

Obviously there was jealousy and the threat of losing my loyalty. Yet when in the house, I was ignored and I played alone. In fact, I frequently was complimented at that age for being the quiet one, yet that reputation, I'm afraid, was not to last for long! But once again, there was a sort of superficial, required notion of family, without anything of substance to back it up. Having any real needs or concerns was somehow antithetical to family, rather than family being the first place you'd turn when in need.

When a sibling dies, the other children may feel guilty for still being alive. And in loveless families, where there is little, if any, honest communication allowed, these feelings go unexpressed, or else these feelings are dismissed when they are expressed. The parents, in turn, may feel resentment toward the living child or children if it was their favorite child who died.

The Effects of Growing Up in a Household That Experiences a Death of a Close Family Member

In a loveless family, you probably were given little, if any, comfort or opportunity to share your feelings. If the person died from a lingering illness, you may not have been told what it was. Perhaps there was an initial day or two of crying permitted, but then that was supposed to be that. So you likely became a more introspective person, learning to trust few, if any, people with your true feelings. Introspection can be a highly valuable tool. It can be the source of creativity, imagination, and new ideas. And if you can find comfort simply within yourself, that, too, can be extremely useful.

However, the problem is that you may have become too much of a loner. Even if superficially you know many people—even if you are famous or have 10 children—there is a great deal that you keep locked inside you. You aren't necessarily afraid to share with others. It may be more that you don't think anyone will understand. Indeed, many people do not know what to say when you talk about experiencing the death of a close family member at a young age. But even when talking about something else, you may keep looking for validation from others that you never seem to get. So after awhile, you give up looking for it.

Though you can be friendly and say the right thing if someone is upset, or tell a joke that makes people laugh, there may be a somewhat distant quality about you. It's possible that you are not known first and foremost for your warmth—someone that people take one look at and want to hug. Some people seem really, really glad to see someone and their warmth fills the room. You probably are not like this. This does not mean you necessarily are nasty and unpleasant, or never feel glad to see someone. But even when hugging an old friend, you are somewhat at arms-length on the inside. You may have even wondered if you actually care very much about anyone. You don't want to be lonely, but you don't want people to get too close, either.

You may even have become a scornful person somewhere along the way. You may have little sympathy yourself for adults as they lose family members. You got through it as a child, so why can't they get through it as adults? You learned at any early age about the inevitability of death, and so you have a rather matter-of-fact outlook on it. Could a 40 year old really have never considered before that eventually her parents will die?

If you try to help the grieving adult anyway by saying something like, "I know what you're going through because my father died when I was 10," it may backfire. Some people may not want to hear that apparently they are less courageous than a 10-year-old child was. So they do not comment on this or make the connection with you that is being offered. And perhaps without realizing it, you *are* being a bit passive-aggressive. On an unconscious level, you may want this person to know that whatever they are going through, you've been through worse.

Particularly if you experienced more than one death while growing up, it may be hard for you to invest much time in other people. You know perfectly well that sooner or later they will die, so you'd rather not keep in touch with a friend who moves away, or break up an intimate relationship without giving it a full chance.

Still, most everyone wants to feel some connection to someone, so it's also possible that you remain fanatically devoted to the few people you know that you can trust. So some people know you as the most loyal friend in the world, while other people know you as someone who routinely drops people without looking back.

Depending on how the person died, you may carry a great deal of hatred inside you. Obviously if someone murdered or caused the accidental death of a family member, it is enormously difficult to make peace within yourself over what happened. In fact, you may well have justification in feeling like you shouldn't have to. If someone tortured, raped, and murdered your child, isn't it perfectly normal to never forgive that person? You should *not* take justice into your own hands, but surely it is understandable if you go to your grave wishing nothing but the worst for that person.

But sometimes people can also grow to hate the person who died—for abandoning them, for leaving them in a precarious situation, for driving drunk, for not taking out a restraining order, for not seeing a doctor sooner, for refusing to quit smoking despite doctor's orders, for taking out his anger in dying on the people trying to help him, for being in denial about death and so making no effort to leave this world with relationships in order, or for any number of things. Even if the person suffered a great deal, you may not feel much sympathy for her. Instead, you may be angry that he's caused you such grief, especially if in theory it could've been avoided.

Since you probably were raised to be very critical of yourself and sometimes barely think you are entitled to any happiness at all, you may be quite confused as to how to process your losses as you go through life. You want to feel sorry for yourself, but you think that is weak and you loathe self-pity, so the death(s) you survived remains in a kind of limbo.

PART FOUR

OVERCOMING THE LOVELESS FAMILY

I do not pretend to have all the answers, but here are some friendly suggestions you might consider.

16

Finding Lasting Friendship

A wonderful thing about friendship is that it involves two people what simply like each other—or yes, even love each other. They do not have to be related, the same age, work in the same field, have the same hobbies, or be of the same religious or ethnic background.[1] They do not have to have the same amount of money or vote the same way. But for whatever reason, Savannah and Keisha like each other. It's an enormous comfort to know that even if you do not feel close to family members or have no friends at work, you can still have people in your life to talk to and do things with. For some people, their friendship network becomes a kind of substitute family—they get from their friends what they didn't get from their actual family.[2] Interestingly, it is an honor when you call a friend brother or when someone is your sorority sister. Yet one's actual brothers or sisters may be far less desirable companions.

Single people with strong friendship networks may be content to remain single and not feel like they *have to* settle down if they do not want to. At the same time, partnered people can find it refreshing to still leave room in their lives for friends, and not to feel bored or smothered by their relationship. Also, of course, friends can be a source for talking about your intimate relationship—just having someone who will listen can make a big difference, and a friend may just offer some sage advice.

But if you grew up in a loveless family, you felt belittled and trivialized. You were raised to be disconnected from people, reveal little of your true self, or fake a closeness you did not really feel. Further, you may well have been discouraged from making friends with people outside the family. You may have been yelled at or made to feel guilty for preferring time spent with your friends to time spent with the family.

It therefore would not be surprising if you have few, if any, close friends. Maybe your only real friend is your significant other, or if you are single, you may be a recluse. But sometimes looks can be deceiving. Even if you are considered a good listener or sympathetic soul, and even if you know many people, underneath it all you may have anxiety and confusion about how to form a platonic bond with another person. You may exaggerate the importance of a minor slight from another person and miss out on getting to know someone worthwhile. Contrastingly, you may tolerate extremely inconsiderate—or dangerous—behavior on the part of another person. When you have a shaky sense of self, it is hard to know who or what will be good for you, who to trust, and what is a normal range of human error versus cruelty. You may even be unsure about who actually likes you and may find it hard to comprehend when someone does.

At a basic level, you may not know what other people are *for*. This is not to say you are conceited. But you may feel like you're *supposed* to have friends, and so you see it as a positive reflection on yourself if you know enough people to give a party, or you get a lot of e-messages or holiday cards. Obviously, the reverse is also true: you get few holiday cards and so forth, and so you make a negative judgment upon yourself—nobody likes me. (When I was a teenager and the world was less computerized, I was obsessed with my address book. I thought a full address book of names and phone numbers would somehow prove something to myself. And I was into my 20s before I stopped automatically asking anyone whom I had had a pleasant time with at a party for their phone number—that I didn't have to try to be lifelong friends with everyone in the world.)

The thing is, you may well feel that you do have something to prove to yourself—that despite the messages you got from your family, you are a full human being just like anyone else, and it's possible for people to like you for who you are. Your life may sometimes seem like a *before* and *after*—before you left home and after you did, which is when your life actually began. (Unless, of course, you have never been able to leave home, despite all the problems associated with it.) It's possible you've had many of these before-and-after transformations of self: before and after you joined a certain religion or before and after you began a therapeutic process. You feel like you started out in life as nothing, and the longer you have distanced yourself from your family, the more of a person you have become.

Another way of trying to prove yourself through other people is to gravitate toward individuals who very much remind you of family members from your past.[3] However, to show yourself how much you've grown and changed, you may go out of your way to connect with such a person so as to demonstrate how much better you can handle this type of situation now. While anything is possible, it may just turn out that you can't handle this person any better than you could before, and your relationship may grow volatile and hateful over time.

But while it certainly can be important to explore the sociable side of yourself, in the final analysis, other people do not exist so you can prove to yourself—or the ghosts of your past—that you are outgoing, confident, and likeable. Over time, you may seem more like a *character* than a person. People expect you to say or do things that are unusual to insure yourself that you are noticed. But it's not the same thing as feeling secure in the knowledge that you are liked. You're noticed all right, yet you don't really feel included.

Keeping up this type of routine can be exhausting—especially when it doesn't seem to accomplish what you want it to. So as you get older, you may stop trying so hard. As this happens, you may find yourself spending more time alone, because when you aren't acting, you don't know what else to do.

This leads to another reason why people may seek out social contacts: loneliness. Having been raised to have little, if any, self-confidence, you may feel lonely or abandoned quite easily. Even if you are well-accustomed to being alone, over time you may feel like: "Enough already. I need to talk to *someone;* I need to feel that there's somebody who cares." And so even if the best you can come up with is someone who you do not really like much or who gets on your nerves, you make do with what crumbs of attention you can get. This might seem better than nothing—and so perhaps it is—but it's still not the same thing as feeling good about your friends. You may still feel lonely even when you are doing things together.

It's also possible that you'll feel resentment or depression—that you're a loser who only attracts losers, because anyone truly worth knowing would not want to spend time with you. So these sour grape, better-than-nothing friendships might reinforce inner feelings of unworthiness and abandonment.

Sometimes, too, people who have little self-esteem think that the only way they can get people to like them is to do things for them.[4] And so they offer favors to other people—whether the other people like it or not. There's nothing wrong with helping people out or buying someone a gift. But sometimes it is overkill. There is not a sense of mutual closeness and so the superficial generosity leaves a bad taste in people's mouths. Or, people being people, they sort of passive–aggressively take advantage of you. There may be people who never contact you and you always have to contact them. They confide their troubles in you or ask you for money, but then exclude you from their social lives.

Another pattern to be wary of is destructive behavior in the name of seeking out friends. If you do not have the courage to attend a social gathering without the benefit of alcohol or drugs, you run the risk of becoming an addict. Or maybe you've concluded that you never will have friends, so you drink or take drugs alone, to pass the time. Or overspend, so that clothes or objects keep you company. Or you decide that though you can't have friends, you can have a lot of sex with strangers, which puts your personal safety at risk. Even when you were a child, you may have made friends with people who taught you bad habits or got you in trouble, because these were the only people who seemed to accept you. And you may continue to make friends with the wrong people as an adult.

In the final analysis, friendship is not about proving anything to anyone, or simply filling up space because you fear your own emptiness. It's about *liking* someone who *likes* you in return. Friendships have ups and downs, and sometimes come to an end. Someone you thought was a friend betrays you, or develops deeper feelings that you do not wish to return, or maybe you simply lose touch. But for the duration of the friendship, the players care about each other and enjoy each other's company.

Whether you're a recluse or you maintain a kind of false popularity, there are some things you can do to try to find genuine friendship.

Who makes you feel good? I recently spoke to someone who complained that a particular network on TV showed too many reruns and that she was tired of watching the same shows over and over. The obvious solution to her problem was...change the channel! (Some might say, better yet, turn off the TV.) But sometimes we do not see what is obvious to other people. So, as basic as it may sound, does your friend(s) make you feel good, or not? Sometimes professional or other situations compel us to spend a fair amount of time with people we don't really like. But if there is nothing at stake, and someone makes you sad or angry instead of happy, you do not have to keep associating with him or her. If you do not feel safe formally ending the connection by explaining why you do not care for the person then just stop returning messages. If it is someone truly unsafe, you should look into getting a restraining order.

Sometimes people are engaging when we are face-to-face with them—or even texting them—but when we think about them afterwards we just don't like them. Maybe you are able to identify why this is, or not. But if you don't enjoy being in communication with someone then look for people for whom this is not the case.

If you have an enjoyable time with someone, and afterwards recall the person fondly, then probably this is someone you'll want to socialize with again.

Is the friendship fair? If you are the only one who is making contact and/or arranging social activities—if essentially the friendship would go away if you stopped working at it—you might consider seeing what happens when you stop contacting the other person. If she or he never gets in touch with you, then you probably have your answer.

Don't expect too much. However you present yourself to the world, you probably have profound needs that not everyone is going to understand or be able to meet. If you or your friend moves away, you may well stay in touch, especially in today's world when distance communication is so easy. But some people, for whatever their reasons, pretty much assume they'll lose touch when someone moves away. If you used to talk on a daily basis, don't assume that will still happen when you live far apart. A best friend might become someone that you now hear from once a year or so. That can be nice for what it is and you can make new friends at the same time.

Also, when people partner up or have children, they often see less of their friends. For that matter, maybe that person has to take care of a sick relative or has gone back to school and has to study a lot. Even people whose lives do not change much may simply socialize less as they get older or they will take on a new hobby that does not involve you. Try not to take it personally when someone seems to be less of a friend because of major changes in her life.

Who doesn't remind you of your family? If you meet someone who reminds you of a family member whom you did not care for, it might be best to stay away. You may have difficulty sorting out your feelings or reacting to the person in constructive ways. You might also think that you can heal old family wounds by using this person as a stand-in for your mother, or brother, or grandmother. It is doubtful this will work as intended and it is also not fair to the other person.

Instead, try to meet people who do *not* remind you of your family. Maybe it is easy to recognize the signs—for example, someone who drinks too much, or gets angry too easily. But even if it takes time for you to make a more subtle connection, put your own needs first. Maybe it's nothing the other person does on purpose, but if you really can't handle someone who lives or believes a certain way, don't take on more than you can handle.

Who isn't dangerous? Again, it may seem so obvious is does not need to be said, but avoid knowing criminals. They are likely to complicate your life in unfortunate ways. Also, anyone with a mental issue that is not in treatment or recovery is more likely to be harmful in some way than people who do not have these issues, or have them under control. You may find your own behavior deteriorating to keep pace with this other person. Or he may put you in the wrong place at the wrong time—for example, you are with him while he gets arrested for illegal drug possession.

Also, if someone has a hobby that you don't feel safe about, trust your instincts. If you're afraid of guns, don't feel you have to accept an invitation to go hunting or target shooting. If you fear heights, don't feel you have to go skydiving. If you're a recovering alcoholic who has trouble being around alcohol, don't feel you have to sit there all night and watch someone drink.

Be yourself. If someone truly likes you, they should be able to accept that you are of a different religion or political affiliation, that you like a different kind of music or movie, that you have different tastes in food or clothing, that you are straight or gay, and so forth. And the same holds true of you in reverse. If you truly cannot accept the fact that this person belongs to Religion X, then look for someone who doesn't. It's unlikely you'll get the person to start believing some other way.

In fact, it's probably not a good idea to get into nasty debates over differing opinions, as you are probably unlikely to change the person's mind. All that may happen is that you'll lose a friend. But there might be some good-natured teasing back and forth over these differences. And maybe even some agreements or a willingness to meet in the middle. You might also mutually appreciate hearing from someone with a point of view that differs from your own.

Don't try to control or be controlled. In loveless families, trying to control other people is often presented as love, so letting yourself be controlled by another person—or trying to control another person yourself—may be the only thing you know. But just as it never worked well in your loveless family—in fact, it may have had the opposite effect of what the controlling person wanted—it will not work with other people.

Obviously, parents must keep a close watch on their children, but this should not be a dehumanizing experience. One's ability to control another person is limited; she must be able to live her own life and make her own mistakes. Otherwise, she is not being treated as a human being. If, as an adult, you know someone who is doing something seriously wrong, you can try to intervene, or if need be contact the police. But if the other person likes cauliflower and you don't, let the person enjoy his cauliflower.

Don't confuse no with abandonment. If after knowing someone for a week or for 20 years they decide they no longer want to be friends, try not to take this as some major abandonment of cosmic proportions. There can be any number of reasons why they are cutting things off, some of which you may agree with, and some of which you may not. But ultimately, everyone has the right to terminate a friendship, even if we ourselves are the ones being terminated. It does *not* mean that no one else will ever like you, that all the mean things your family used to say about you are true, or anything of the sort. Not all relationships are destined to last throughout the life course. There doubtless are people who have expressed a lack of interest toward the friend who stops being your friend. These things happen to everyone.

Be able to enjoy your own company. If you enjoy being alone but still want to see someone socially, then you know you really like that person. If, however, you are (for example) tired from work or bordering on getting the flu and want nothing more than to crawl into bed and read or watch a movie, a genuine friend should be able to understand that you won't be able to go bowling or go out to dinner after all. A certain amount of time to one's self in a given day can be recuperative or even inspirational. Fear of abandonment should not make you feel forced to participate in a minor social event that you're just not in the mood for. In other words, to use a highly overused cliché, if you do not like yourself, no one else will like you either. So ironically, part of maintaining healthy friendships is being able to maintain enjoyable moments alone. Otherwise, your friendships might be somewhat disingenuous. You simply are afraid to be alone, or worry that you'll have a reputation for being unpopular.

Occasionally there are people who consciously decide that they are happier or more true to themselves by having little, if any, contact with others. But most people have a genuine desire to connect. If weeks, or months, or even years go by without having friendly interactions with at least one person, you have every right to feel lonely—and to do something about it.

But if you are afraid to be alone at all—if seven days out of seven you must constantly be around people—you have issues that probably should be dealt with in a professional setting. Even in recovery programs that emphasize daily meetings, ideally you still should be able to entertain yourself for a few hours here and there in a given day.

Without doing anything illegal or dangerous, or overspending your budget, find hobbies or activities that you truly enjoy with yourself. Even if it's just taking a bubble bath or dancing around the room to your favorite song.

There are times in which we all benefit from sharing our woes with a friend. But if you lack the inner skills to self-heal at all, again you should strongly consider consulting a professional.

17

Finding Lasting Intimacy

Increasingly in our society, people choose to remain single.[1] Maybe they have a part-time relationship that fulfills their needs or maybe they prefer to be unattached. If, whatever your arrangement, you feel you have something that works for you, you may decide to skip this chapter. But if you want a sustained, healthy relationship but have not had much success with finding a relationship at all—or finding a healthy one, or one that lasts—you may want to consider if feeling unloved while growing up is part of the reason why. Or, if you've been aware of this for some time, to think about it some more.

It may seem too obvious to even mention, but just in case: intimacy can include sex, but sex is not the only thing that goes into intimacy. I know many happy couples who do not have particularly active sex lives or who confide that the person they chose to settle down with was not the best sex partner that they ever had. Still, to give brief nod to sex: if you are trying to find intimacy solely through sex, you probably will not achieve your goal. If you enjoy recreational sex with multiple partners and follow safe-sex practices, that's your choice. But if you have sex quite often—or with many different people—simply to keep loneliness or depression at bay, you may want to consult a psychologist or psychiatrist about finding a better solution. This is especially true if you are doing things that are unsafe or that make you uncomfortable, just so you please another person. And people who grow up in loveless families are prone to fear displeasing someone. Obviously, too, if you are unable to perform sex, or are afraid of it, or you hate it for some reason, you again should see a doctor.

In any case, *intimacy* herein means honest bonding with another person. How much of that bonding includes sex is something for you to decide. Friendship can also be a form of intimacy—and a form of love. You are intimate with another person when the two of you have exchanged honesty and acknowledge each other as full-fledged human beings, warts and all. Intimacy can occur for only a short duration—some people say that they've had one-night stands that were truly intimate—but in this chapter we'll be talking more about long-term, lasting intimacy, whether legally married or not. And this can be difficult to achieve if (a) you do not recognize your own dignity as a human being, and/or (b) you were never taught how to recognize the human dignity of another person.

No one ever fully knows another person.[2] There are always thoughts, feelings, and memories that people keep to themselves. Even when we do share with others, we might tell the same story differently over time, or leave out certain details. And also, of course, sometimes people share something that is not true, or is biased or delusional. So at best, we know quite a lot about another person, but never everything.

That our knowledge of other people will always be limited has interesting implications in regard to intimacy. One is that a given individual is *always* more than who we see her to be, even if she is a best friend, life partner, or one's identical twin. No one is *just* a breadwinner, a homemaker, a celebrity, a child, a homeless person, a president, a singer, or a convict. Even if you think of someone as the love of your life or soul mate, that person is still other things as well.

To keep track of our complex lives, we often assign the people we encounter with specific roles.[3] Some roles may be extremely short-lived, such as someone who waits on you in a store. But that person has his own complicated existence beyond saying, "May I help you?" or "Here's your change." But you probably just think of him as a store clerk, because that's all you need to know about him. Yet even if you live with someone for 50 years as life partner, he or she will still get somewhat compartmentalized in your mind. When a life partner suddenly wants to split up, or leave you for someone else, or gets seriously ill, or dies, it is a painful reminder that other people are beyond our control. Your soul mate is her own person, not just an abstraction or object.

Lifelong relationships become harder to achieve as the world we live in becomes ever more complex. There are many options other than staying together if you are unhappy, and indeed, many people pursue these other options. It's a well-known fact that the divorce rate in the United States is about 50 percent.[4]

In short, you can come from a close, loving family and—for any number of reasons—never find a satisfactory intimate relationship. And it's also true that you can come from a loveless family and find someone who truly makes you a happier and better person for the rest of your life. But it may well prove harder to achieve this goal if, in fact, you were never taught how to give or receive love. You may even have difficulty accepting the fact that you are entitled to the same forms of happiness that other people are, because you may lack the self-esteem to realize you are another person just like everyone else. Your issues may include:

An expectation of non-validation or abandonment. If the act of growing up—of no longer being a cute baby—was more trouble than your family thought it was worth, you may have come to expect that anything you have to say will be dismissed as wrong. (Were you ever told while growing up, "Why can't you be the way you were when you were a baby, or when you were three, or whatever?" In other words, the person you are growing into for the rest of your life is unacceptable.) If you said something too extreme for their ears, or maybe got caught doing something they did not approve of, you may have been disowned. The message is that other people can express their viewpoints, but not you. Other people can express disagreement, but not you. Other people can be sad or angry, but not you.

So even if your partner says or does something that hurts you deeply or really gets on your nerves, you never say anything. Maybe he or she does something sexually that you actually find revolting, but you don't say anything about it. If he or she says something you think is wrong, you do not offer a dissenting point of view. This can be the kind of relationship that looks good to the outside world, and then suddenly people are shocked to hear the couple split up—or that there was violence, even murder—because either or both people reached a point where they couldn't keep lying and pretending.

Looking for family substitutes. There is no way to go back in time. Yet some people decide that the next best thing is to pick someone for an intimate partner that in some way represents the past. This could be a cultural characteristic, a physical resemblance, a career, or even small things like coming from the same geographic region you grew up in or having the name of a family member. Supposedly, by making this present relationship work, the past will be healed. This may happen consciously or unconsciously.

Well, anything is possible. Maybe you will reach a point where you no longer have a bad reaction when hearing words that bring back unpleasant family memories, be they *Swedish American, certified public accountant,* or *New Jersey.* But if you are expecting another person to be a cure-all, that simply will not happen. Again, no other person will ever know you completely. And in a way, you are treating the other person like an object—he or she *exists* to make you feel better about your past.

Not being true to yourself. Although many people do not like or get along with their families, many people also internalize the values and beliefs they were taught. If your grew up in a family where there was prejudice against certain kinds of people, you may have to do some inner work to fully get beyond those prejudices. Prejudice can take many forms, the more obvious ones being racial–ethnic and gender. But some people are prejudiced against poor people, gay people, or someone from a different political party or religion. Or maybe your family thought you had to be a doctor, or lawyer, or business executive, and that if you weren't you'd turn into a bum in their eyes—even if you made good money doing something else. So, despite having distanced yourself from your family, it still may seem like you can hear their disapproval, even when you haven't told them what you've done that they would not approve of.

Thus, you marry a Catholic you don't love just to keep your Catholic family happy. Or a Republican. Or a Democrat. Or someone who has a certain profession. Or maybe you are gay but marry someone of the opposite sex to please your family. But the question must be posed: what kind of happiness is it when *you* are unhappy for not being true to yourself? One hears about royal families who have rigid expectations as to how family members live and marry. But chances are your family is not royalty. It just seems to think that it is. If you supposedly broke your father's heart by marrying a Jew instead of a Protestant, you may want to pose the question: "What about *my* heart?" Some families are still extremely old-fashioned about a woman having a career outside the house upon getting married or having children. They decide that this is a bad woman for continuing to work when she has a baby. This is really nobody's business but the woman's—and her partner, if she has one.

Expecting your partner to heal you. In real life, there are no Prince or Princess Charmings. No one can just say *abracadabra* and make all your pain and anger go away. Another person can *help*, but he cannot cure. It can be important to share your family horror stories with your partner. But this should be to help her get to know you better. She can offer loving gestures, and express sympathy, and take your side, all of which can be empowering and feel mighty nice. But she can't undo a lifetime of negative messages.

Testing the other person's boundaries. If you were never allowed to be a bad boy or girl while growing up—if anything less than perfect behavior at all times made for excessive punishment or belittling— you may at times behave childishly, or do something that you know is wrong. You want to see if your partner is a substitute mom or dad who will let you be bad and still love you. Maybe you unconsciously squeeze the toothpaste tube from the middle just to know that you can do it without getting the crap beaten out of you. Couples often engage in playful teasing, and no matter what your age, there may be a pleasant element of the childlike in your relationship—it's no coincidence that one's partner might be called one's baby. But there's a difference between having a tickle fight and, say, having multiple affairs, or losing the mortgage. There's bad and then there's *bad*. If your testing of someone's boundaries starts to involve real harm to that person or yourself, you would benefit by seeing a relationship counselor.

Not as awful as your family, so what's the problem? If you grew up in a household where people lost their tempers on a daily basis, you may think there's nothing the matter, because you only lose your temper a couple of times a week. What you're dishing out to your partner perhaps barely scratches the surface of what you went through, so you are hurt and baffled if your partner says you make him feel unsafe, or that you have hurt her feelings. Some people grow up never getting yelled at or beaten. Nobody went around breaking household objects out of anger and all family members were treated as equals. And so what to you is a small or infrequent burst of bad temper or insults is to your partner the worst experience he ever had. If your partner came from a good, happy family and you resent this, you may need to reconsider your relationship or seek professional help.

Breaking up before your partner does. Whether it's a genuine concern or an unfounded fear in your own mind, you may decide that your partner is about to break up with you. So rather than feel abandoned again, you decide to do the abandoning yourself. Or maybe it's not about completely breaking up, but just not being there for the other person when she feels she really needs you. After all, where was she last year when you were dealing with some problem of your own? If your relationship starts turning into a contest as to who can out-abandon the other, again seek counseling.

If you want a long-term, healthy, intimate relationship, but are unable to even come close to this goal, there is professional help available, as well as many books that can offer practical advice. Here are just a few of many things you might consider:

Try different ways of meeting people. If you are still carrying around old family baggage that tells you that you aren't worth the trouble, no one will ever like you, or maybe even just a general inertia or despair that permeated your home while growing up, you may get into a rut where years go by, and you never even try to meet someone. Or maybe you think things like online dating services are beneath you, or that you'd be embarrassed to even try such a thing. But in today's world many perfectly respectable people trying to live happy and confident lives may pursue (for example) an online dating service, or other Internet sites, to meet someone special. (Of course, you want to be careful about connecting with someone before actually meeting her or him, and you don't want to do anything illegal.) But also, don't be afraid to say to your friends, "Do you work with anyone single that I might like?" Or join a hobby club in your community, a support group, or a political organization. If you're religious, get involved in a place of worship. But you need to get out there and *try*. You need to know that you're worth the effort.

Do not pursue unviable people. If you're gay, don't assume a straight person is actually a closet case. If you're straight, don't think you can make a gay person fall in love with you. While sometimes, yes, partnered people will break up their relationships to get together with someone new, quite often they don't. They often prefer just to keep you off to the side as a secret. While some people can handle having these kinds of affairs, if you cannot—if it makes you hurt and angry to be second best in the person's life—don't put yourself in that situation. Also, if someone broke up with their spouse to be with you, there's a chance that in the future they will break up with *you* to be with someone else. Maybe this will not happen and you'll stay together as a happy couple. But if someone has done something before, there's always the chance she'll do it again.

If you come from a loveless family, you may feel like you're proving something important to yourself if you get someone to end his marriage to be with you. Or if you supposedly turn a straight person gay or a gay person straight, because he or she just loves *you* so much that it doesn't even matter if you're a woman or a man. Or maybe your family disowned you for being gay. (Of course, some people are genuinely bisexual, but that is not the scenario at hand.) But such efforts are at least as likely to fail as to succeed, and you may create a great deal of pain for yourself and other people.

Don't overwhelm the other person with your past. On the one hand, you should not keep your unhappy childhood a secret from your partner. This person needs to get to know the real you. But timing can be important here. If, on a first date, you tell someone something like, "My father went to prison for beating my mother," you may be sending out the wrong message. Your date may think you are damaged goods—that if right off the top you talk about something so traumatic, what else awaits? Also, your date may have no idea how to respond to something so unexpected, and so his or her response disappoints you, and you decide too quickly that this person cannot meet your emotional needs. Share, but do it at a comfortable pace.

Find someone trustworthy. If someone's stories about themselves do not add up—if there are obvious contradictions—it certainly could be that this is a dishonest person. To simplify, someone tells you he is a successful stockbroker, but has no money to pay for his dinner. *Something* is not right. If someone is always late, changes her stories from one meeting to the next, shares a secret that he promised not to tell anyone about, moves faster than you are comfortable with sexually—these, and many other examples, may well indicate that this is someone you cannot trust. She may be appealing to you in other ways, but apparently she does not tell the truth very often, or listen to what you have to say.

Someone you enjoy spending time with. Just because someone has a pulse and is interested in you does not mean you are required to be interested in her or him in return. If you do not enjoy the person's company, if it's never really fun and more like an ordeal you endure, and you can't wait until it's over—and this can include sex—you need to remind yourself that you deserve better. (A variation on this is to meet someone who is your physical ideal, and to assume this means you were meant to be soul mates, even though you don't enjoy each other's company.) Also, if the person makes you uncomfortable by always interrupting you when you're talking, or always trying to control situations, you probably aren't having much fun, either. Sometimes people grow fonder of each other over time, but if you are more unhappy being with this person than being alone, find the courage to be alone.

Stay away from fixers. Some people think they have all the answers, or it makes them feel better about themselves if their partner is a more messed up person than they are. Not only should you avoid wanting someone to fix you, but you should avoid people who want to fix you. It's often evident early on if (for example) someone is always giving you advice but never wants advice in return. Some people *want* to be put on pedestals, and such relationships are likely to end extremely unhappily. People raised in loveless families can be vulnerable to these fixers. Be clear within yourself that you want a partner, not a parent.

Sexual boundaries and needs. It is possible to have a successful and happy long-term relationship even if you and your partner are not a perfect fit, sexually speaking. But it takes communication and compromise. If your partner does things sexually that make you feel emotionally or physically uncomfortable, are unsafe, or simply do not turn you on, you need to have a serious discussion. This can be difficult if you are unaccustomed to speaking up for yourself—or even think you have the right to do so. You may even have trouble saying something like, "You're hurting my elbow." Again, perhaps a visit to a couples' therapist is in order. In return, you need not automatically feel depressed or abandoned if your partner likewise says he or she does not like something you're doing.

Find a balance of time together and apart. Even if you are living under the same roof—or *especially* if you are—you need to feel secure enough within yourself to be happy when your partner is out of town, or even just at work. If you still are suffering major wounds from growing up in a loveless family, this may be easier said than done. While dating, if you get frightened or depressed because someone hasn't called back at the exact moment he said he would, it's possible you are not ready yet for a long-term healthy relationship. Of course, it could also be that you are dating someone, and the person is not good for you, or it's just not working out, but you don't want to admit it. But if you reach the live-in stage, it should not be a big deal if (for example) one night a week your partner has some kind of group activity that does not involve you. In fact, over the long term, these little breaks from each other may actually help the relationship to thrive. But you need to be in a secure enough state of heart and mind to accept this.

Understand it takes work. Great relationships don't just fall form the sky. Even if you and your partner become quite happy with each other in a relatively short amount of time, life inevitably presents people with hardships and disappointments. Whether it be incompatible daily habits or major upheavals, you may well have to be willing to make an ongoing commitment to work things out—and see a relationship counselor if need be. Even couples who live happily together for a lifetime experience moments in which either or both parties wonder if they'd be better off breaking up.

If you come from a loveless family, you may think that someone will just instantly make your life better because you deserve it after being so unhappy. But again, this person has his or her own life agenda, and does not exist only to help you. And the other person may well need some help from you sometimes, too. You may also think that this relationship simply has to last because you cannot stand any more heartbreak or abandonment. This is not the best reason for staying together, but even as such, if you want it to keep working, you may have to do some work yourself.

18

Relating to Children

Some people who never felt they had love, patience, or understanding as children are able to give their own children these things they never had themselves.[1] Perhaps they have done some work to improve their own characters, or perhaps the balance between the cognitive and emotional within themselves simply gives them a clear sense of priorities.

But many parents find it difficult to give things they never had.[2] A parent may vow, "No child of mine will ever have to go through such-and-such like I did with my family," but then in actual practice, the parent does more or less the same things with his own child. That the parent may do it *less* than was done to them will not make a difference to the child. The children may still end up thinking you're a monster, even if—as you might have done yourself as a child—they never tell you.

In addition to not being able to give something you never had, you might have internalized some of the values—or should we say lack of values?—you were raised with. So as much as you hated being yelled at or hit, you see a child act out and think, "That spoiled brat should get yelled at and hit." We also tend to model our own behavior on those around us, even when we do not want to, especially when we have little self-esteem or sense of how to live. You may also be too obsessed with your own past to spend enough time in the present and give a child the proper amount of attention. Further, you may simultaneously give your child things you never had *and* resent the child for not being grateful enough or not comprehending your secret pain.

Still other people use their children to sort of erase their own childhoods. And so the children grow up with little, if any, sense of boundaries.[3] The parent strives to be a best friend instead of a parent and the child ends up finding life difficult in other ways. She was never prepared to face disappointment, or be told no. And so she is a difficult person to work with or to know on a personal level. In extreme cases, such children may grow up to commit murder, since, after all, they were raised to think they could get away with it.

Since loveless families often are also clueless families, oddly enough, you may feel a lot of pressure from relatives to have children. Someone may insist that you were born to be a mother, or that if any man should have children, it should be you, or, that you have so much love to give. And if you *do* want to have children, that of course is your choice. But if you have doubts—if you aren't sure you will be able to break free of at least some of the negativity you grew up with—you may want to think twice about having children. If you are inclined to criminal behavior, have difficulty controlling your addiction(s), go from one intimate relationship to another, lack patience, have a volatile temper, or have diagnosable mental conditions, you may especially want to think carefully as to whether having children is something you can or should take on.

It would be nice if I could say with honesty, "Don't be silly, just have kids, no parent is perfect." Or if I could say: "Here is the blueprint for raising happy and well-adjusted children despite the abuses you suffered yourself." But unfortunately, I can say neither. Maybe, despite what others say, you really *aren't* going to be a good mother or father. No one is good at everything. And if you actually harbor conscious fears that you may not have the love and patience required for raising a child, you should not feel like you *have to* have children nonetheless.

I am not being sarcastic or belittling when I say that you may be better off sticking to having a pet. Many people find deep bonds of love with their pets. But maybe you are unable to meet the challenge of taking care of an animal, and neglect, abandon, or abuse the creature. (In which case you shouldn't have pets, either.) Talking good care of any living thing requires empathy and patience. Some people get enraged when a cat hisses like a cat or a dog barks because that's what dogs do. Indeed, this might be a good question to ask yourself: if you've neglected, abused, or abandoned an animal, do you think you can handle raising a child? If you flushed your goldfish down the toilet because it was too much trouble to feed it, do you think you can take on a human being for the next 18 years? Some people find watering a houseplant too much trouble. Again, my point is not to be critical, but realistic.

Even more to the point, if you know people with children but take little interest in them—if you feel they are a nuisance when they come into the room, can barely say hello to them, and can't wait until they leave—you again should seriously consider whether or not you should become a parent yourself. Even the best of parents appreciate a break away from their children. But if spending time with a child or teenager makes you feel like you're in prison, again, parenting may not be for you.

People sometimes make clever jokes about not liking kids. Yet beneath the brittle sophistication of such remarks, there often is an adult who is still smarting over her own childhood. Each of us starts out as a child and has many primal experiences as a child. So if you hate children, you are hating something that you used to be yourself—you are hating a part of yourself and your own life experience. If you cannot get past these feelings—and some people can't, even after years of therapy—you may be better off accepting your limitations, and not experimenting on an actual child to see if the child's technical existence will heal you. Just as you are not merely an it or a thing, neither is a child.

If you have one or more children and are a loving and wise parent who truly treasures time with your children—even if sometimes they make it hard to do so!—you deserve much praise. You did a difficult thing: you were able to get past your own issues to truly care for this human life you are responsible for. No parent is ever perfect, and since people are complex creatures, no child ever turns out 100 percent the way the parents wanted her to. You may even have moments in which your own painful memories of neglect or abuse make it challenging for you to spare your child these same conditions. Heck, maybe you even mess up now and then and overreact—or under-react, as the case may be. But if, on balance, you and your children love and trust each other, and your children do at least reasonably well at making appropriate friends, obeying family rules (though of course there is always some rebellion), and are doing well in school and other activities, you have a lot to be proud of.

At the same time, no matter how hard you try, sometimes children pick up on your own unresolved issues. Just because something happened a long time ago, you may still be the same kind of person you were then. Despite your warnings to your daughter, she gets pregnant as a teenager just like you did. If you were a suicidal youth, then tragically your own child may be suicidal. If you were a terrible student and your parents couldn't get you to do your homework no matter how much they yelled and screamed, you may have the same problems with your own children. (Yelling and screaming at someone, even another adult, usually just frightens them, and seldom has the desired effect.)

Some emotional traits—including depression—may be genetic. But children can be more observant and sensitive than they are given credit for. If you are unhappy or impatient, your children may notice it, and learn to be the same way through imitation. So if you never have the patience to finish what you start—or if you're pretty much a couch potato and don't even try to start anything—don't be too alarmed if your children don't see why they have to do their homework. If you often feel that on the inside you are hanging on by a thread and barely see the point of anything, don't be shocked if your children act out in inappropriate ways. If you're too preoccupied or impatient to give them the emotional support they need, don't be surprised if they turn to other people—or maybe substance abuse—for this support.

Further, children of course change a great deal from infancy to being a teenager. It could be that your child reminds you in a negative way of yourself at a certain age, and rather than face the pain, you belittle the child as a means of belittling that person you used to be. If your child reminds you of a bullying sibling, or one you were always envious of, you may decide to get revenge through the child. It may also be that you have developed certain personality traits or disorders that make it difficult for you to deal with the nature of physical characteristics of a child at a certain stage. Perhaps pre-adolescents gross you out—the children aren't cute anymore.

If you have obsessive–compulsive disorder (OCD) or any number of phobias, you may have an extremely difficult time warming up to your children when they are dirty or do not pick up after themselves. Dirty fingerprints on a wall do not just need to be cleaned off—perhaps for you it is truly disgusting, signaling germs or imperfection. Not to mention things like changing diapers, cleaning up vomit, cleaning a child's nose, and so on. While many people take these tasks in stride, some people can't.

If you expect—or demand—that your children treat you better than other people have, you may be in for a major disappointment. Kids and teens are not yet fully matured, so if adults get on your nerves, or never seem to listen to you, or make fun of you, it is entirely possible that in some phases of their development they will do the same. Yes, you pay the bills, and make their meals, and do hundreds of things for them, but children do not necessarily take this into account. That's just the way it is. If you are thinking that having a child will mean you'll finally get the respect you deserve, you may want to think again. If a teenager says, "Mom, can I borrow the car tonight?" and Mom says no, the teenager is highly *unlikely* to reply, "That's okay, I know you gave birth to me and provided for all my needs for the past 16 years, so I'm happy to do whatever you say."

Ironically, problems raising your own children might have a positive effect: you can see for yourself how difficult parenting can be.[4] But some people never make this connection. To be introspective, you have to have a sense of self, and the healthy confidence to not fear admitting you make mistakes. Many people from loveless families lack these qualities and so the same patterns get repeated one generation after another.

I do not have children. For what it is worth, in my lifetime I have been told I am very good with children and that I am not good with children at all. As a college professor, I have found that some students find me to be extremely helpful and supportive, while others have found me to be intimidating. But even if I were Father of the Year, I would not pretend that a few pages of a book will tell you everything you need to know as a parent—especially if you had a rough childhood yourself. By all means consult many books, join support groups, seek professional guidance—and even then don't be surprised if something between you and your child does not go well.

If you are an outright abusive or neglectful parent, you absolutely should consult a professional, and also consult with your local government office that deals with children's needs. Whatever you've been through, and however much it warrants sympathy, a child should not suffer abuse or neglect at your hands.[5] If you know of someone else who abuses his or her children, you can call the national child-abuse hotline at 1–800–4-A-CHILD.

Try to remember. When some people leave their youth behind, they *really* leave it behind—perhaps because it was so painful. But try to remember things that made you feel embarrassed, hurt, or unloved. Did *you* like it when the grown-ups ignored you, overly criticized you, or never listened to your side of a story? Did *you* like having to kiss Aunt So-and-So when you didn't like her or even know her? Did *you* like it when your parents said, "When I was your age, we listened to *good* music?" Were *you* a model teenager who got straight As, regularly attended a place of worship by choice, and never disobeyed your parents? Did you never drink underage or use illegal drugs? Did you have sex before reaching your legal maturity?...The list goes on and on.

Yes, children need to be guided and disciplined. But ideally this is carried out in a spirit of wanting the child to be a better person, and in a manner that indicates that you still love the child. In fact:

You are not the child's best friend. Children need to be taught that there are boundaries in life, and that there are acceptable and unacceptable life choices to be made. Some parents go to the opposite extreme and do little to constructively help build the child's character. They instead want to be the child's best friend. Such parents often are determined that their child will not have to go through what they went through themselves in their loveless families. So they never set any parameters at all. The child is never made to do anything she doesn't want to do. Though such a child may be the envy of other kids at school, over time the child may look back on the experience as parental negligence, and be just as resentful as children who were overly disciplined. It is impossible to be a well-integrated adult if you have no sense at all that from time to time everyone has to do things they'd rather not do. So the child ends up (for example) dropping out of high school, and since the parents do not want to risk coming off as rigid, they do nothing to stop it. Beneath this extremely relaxed approach to parenting is the same familiar issue of not recognizing your child as a *person*. He exists to make his own way in life. He does not exist to be a psychological tool for healing your own past.

Discipline not abuse. When the child has done nothing to be physically or emotionally harmed but is harmed nonetheless, it is obvious to most people that this is child abuse. But what about when a child has done something to merit some form of reprimand?

Abuse, by definition, is excessive. And *excessive* means more than what is needed. So yes, children need to be disciplined, but they do not need nor will they benefit from *excessive* discipline. The punishment must fit the crime. If the punishment is excessive, it can be labeled abusive.

What is *acceptable* versus excessive discipline? Different cultures have varying practices and standards for how to discipline children, so there are some practices that may be considered normal in one part of the world, but abusive in another. And since raising a child does not come with a blueprint, it's normal for parents to wonder if the punishment they have given is too much or too little. There is an increasing belief that corporal punishment—physically striking a child—never should be practiced, not even a little spanking on the rear end. Yet there are others who balk at this notion and say it represents a cultural bias.

One's own subjective experience may also come into play. I have spoken to people who say they wish they had been spanked, because instead their parents yelled and screamed at them so much that a spanking would have been less toxic. Yet I also have spoken to people who were spanked who say they wished they'd been yelled at instead.

In any event, there is an obvious world of difference between (for example) sending a child to her room with no dessert and starving her. I personally agree that corporal punishment is wrong. But if, for the sake of argument, it is okay to give your child a light smack on the hand, that obviously is quite different from beating him black and blue. Many parents practice the familiar time-out model, in which everyone calms down for a few minutes before going any further. This certainly is more acceptable than shouting cruel remarks to the child that can be wounding in a different way from physical abuse: "I wish you were never born."

Nor should some household rule or policy seem more important than the child herself. Is a wet towel hung in the wrong place really more important than the child's life? If you felt that way yourself growing up, try to remember this when dealing with the situation.

No favorites. Years ago on a bus, I noticed two boys with the person I presume was their mother. They were the same size and dressed in identical clothes—I guessed that they were fraternal twins. They looked about seven years old and each had a balloon. One of the boys had thick golden curls and was extremely animated. He kept saying, "Oh look at that, isn't it wonderful?" or "Tonight will you read us a story?" The boy seemed to have a good vocabulary for his age and great deal of natural enthusiasm for life. Like a kind of boy version of Shirley Temple, he seemed to light up the room—or in this case, the bus. He and the woman kept exchanging kisses because he was so affectionate.

The boy whom I presumed to be his brother had straight brown hair and said barely a word. He kept looking down at the floor while his brother dominated the bus ride. He didn't even hold his balloon with much enthusiasm, though it appeared obvious that he was thinking about something. If the other boy was like the sun, this boy was like the moon.

These children came and went out of my life in about 15 minutes, yet for some reason I've always remembered them. I wondered then—and wonder now—if the parent(s) couldn't help but pay more attention to the lively boy. Or if the quieter boy was favored because he seemed to need more attention. Or if both were loved equally for who they were—rather like one being the sun, the other the moon.

Of course I have no idea of who these children were or who they became before or after the bus ride. But parental figures often find themselves more drawn to one of their children than another. Sometimes this is just human nature at work—one child feels more affinity with Parent A, while another child is closer to Parent B. In a loving family, it can be taken for granted that while yes, everyone loves everyone, Mom and Bob seem to have an especially close connection. And when multiple people, regardless of age, are living under the same roof, there are going to be some rough patches sometimes. If one child is more intelligent, more ambitious, more talented, or a better athlete than another—or to top it off becomes famous—it is not hard to see how parents may find it challenging to make sure their other children do not feel neglected, while still giving the exceptional child the praise he deserves. Of course, the same can also happen when one of the children is mentally or physically different.

But sometimes a parent favors one child over another for more selfish reasons. One child looks too much like the father's ex-wife. One child takes care of mom when she passes out, while the other tries to escape the house. One child has trouble doing well in school and the parents think that makes them look like bad parents. One child is the parent's biological child, but the other isn't, and this makes a difference over time, because the non-biological child is seen as not reflecting the parents in the same way. Or maybe a parent practices the divide-and-conquer strategy. A woman wants to alienate her children from their father, but one of the daughters remains loyal to him, so mom starts to distance herself from her.

Since it is often extremely challenging to give each child an appropriate amount of love and attention, you may consider family therapy if the dynamics with your children are out of balance.

Kids aren't adults. Some people get extremely frustrated—and take it personally—when children act like children. It's like expecting a dog never to bark. Even the most exemplary of children will test their boundaries with you, hide things from you, laugh at an inappropriate time, show an annoying lack of empathy in certain situations, and in general be...well, immature. They're supposed to be immature. They're *children.*

By all means guide them through the land mines of morality and point out why (for example) it's never good to make fun of someone else. But don't expect them to prefer sushi over hamburgers, Shakespeare over *Star Wars,* or to comprehend why there are so many problems in the world. Many adults don't know why life is the way it is themselves. If all the kids like a certain kind of music or want to dress a certain way, and there is nothing toxic in any of this, let your kids fit in. Don't expect your 12-year-old child to be a little adult.

Your kids aren't you. While much family baggage can be carried on from one generation to another, each of us is still his or her own person. Even if Dad is an alcoholic and so is Junior, they are not the exact same person. They may have different needs, different reasons for drinking, different outlooks on life, and may need to do different things to improve themselves. This may seem obvious, but people sometimes don't know this, or they know it in theory and then forget it in actual practice.

Some people, in general, have little sense of being separate beings from others. If she is happy, everyone else must be happy, whether they like it or not. If she is angry or sad, no one else is allowed to be happy.

Some parents decide that their child is going to get piano lessons because the parents wished they could've had them when they were young—even if their child isn't interested. Or the parents take it as a sign of betrayal if the children like grandma but the parents don't, or the children have different political opinions or personal tastes. Again, if the parents felt like no one ever listened to them when they were young, they may feel hurt when their children do not follow the parent's advice, or don't want to be a college professor or wine maker just like the parents.

Things that frightened you when you were young are a source of interest or pleasure for your children—or vice versa. Your favorite food may be something your children can't stand. Maybe you're a man who wasn't sexually experienced with women until you were 20—so if your 18-year-old son says he's gay, you tell him, "Just wait until you're 20, and you'll meet the right girl." Wrong! Let him find his own way, and if you teach him anything, it should be about safe sexual practices. Whether he ends up with a woman, a man, or no one, is up to him. You cannot and should not live his life for him.

Over-protective. Obviously, good parents do very much to look out for their children's well-being. If your 14-year-old daughter says, "I want to go to a sleepover at Susie's house," you have every right to ask, and indeed should ask, "Who is Susie?" And don't stop there. Talk to Susie's parent(s), find out what exactly is going to happen, and how the children will be monitored. When you drive your daughter to Susie's make sure it is a safe environment. In today's world, you can even go online and in minutes find out if one of Susie's family members is a registered sex offender.

But if, in the final analysis, it is reasonable to conclude that your daughter will safely return home the next day without having broken the law or faced any danger the previous evening, then let her go to Susie's. That is being a *protective* parent. For that matter, perhaps you think 14 is too young for a sleepover, and she should wait until she's 15. That's your choice.

By contrast, an *over*protective parent might say something like, "Susie? Who's Susie? Oh my God, you're going to get raped, or killed, or something, I just know it. It's not safe out there. Not only are you not going to Susie's, but I am never going to let you out of my sight for a moment." Having been raised in a loveless family, the parent wants to spare her child all the pain and suffering the parent had to endure as a youth. Yesterday's unloved child has emerged as today's frightened and disoriented mother. And so anything and everything may be off limits: "No you can't take swimming lessons, you'll drown," "You can't learn to drive, you'll have an accident," or "You can't go out on a date, you'll get raped."

This same parent probably also lives in terror of being alone. So she may be more worried about herself than her daughter. Yes, unfortunately young people do get raped on dates, but it is possible to communicate and create a dating policy that minimizes this horrific scenario.

It is only natural to be nervous if your child takes up a high-risk sport or hobby, and it is perfectly reasonable to do some research before permitting your child to engage in it. Any parent with a child serving her or his country in times of war righteously will be anxious. But while terrible things can happen to anyone just walking down the street, your children, as they get older, need to get out into the world and test themselves.

Otherwise, you may be treating your child like a stuffed animal or your personal security blanket. In other words, you are turning him into an it or a thing instead of a separate human being with his own destiny to fulfill.

Kids are more important than household rules. When people are not raised to give and receive love, they may turn into adults with little patience for missteps. They take it personally and assume others do not love, like, or respect them when the rules they have set down are not followed—maybe never even recognized. Also, people who feel unloved may be overly introspective. Their only true friend is their own self, and so when they decide (for example) that this is the way to fold the dishrag on the faucet, it seems a decision of profoundest magnitude that engulfs the entire universe. And so when a 12- or 14-year-old child or teenager puts the dishrag crookedly on the faucet or doesn't ring it out enough, the child might just as well have become a serial killer.

While there should be household rules—and consequences when children do not follow them—the rules need to be kept in perspective. First, rules should have a good reason for existing. Of course you don't want moldy towels, or paint splatters in your carpeting. And of course you want your children to be safe, clean, and responsible. If your children must finish their homework after school before they can play, good for you.

But arbitrary rules that are nothing but your own quirky preferences simply will not mean as much to others as they do to you. For example, does it really matter *that* much if the soap is on the left- or right-hand side of the sink? And again, since youth by definition still have some growing up to do, there are some things they do not appreciate as much as adults often do. For example, the battle over a teenager's messy bedroom is hardly new. While adults often appreciate the aesthetics and practicality of a tidy room, kids just as often do not. Wanting to stay out later than allowed, curiosity over sex, preferring to be with their clique of friends than with their little sister—these sorts of issues are inevitable. And by all means read books, talk to people whose opinions you value—maybe even yes, ask your children themselves for input—and do your best to create a loving and livable household. But keep these household policies in perspective. Some may well be a matter of life and death, but others may just be about letting your kids know who's boss. If your underage, intoxicated teen drives the car without permission and wrecks it, that's extremely serious. It is in the teen's best interests to make sure he has serious consequences to pay. Also consider family therapy. But the consequences of forgetting to

hang up a bath towel should not be just as severe. Yet in loveless families, such may be the case. In fact, the punishment for the wet towel
might even be worse, because the car accident signals that the child
needs more serious attention than anyone is willing to give her. In a
loving family, even if the child is made to pay seriously for an offence,
the child still knows she is loved.

Be consistent. Superficially, loveless families sometimes—though
not always—actually seem like more fun than loving families. While
sometimes unloved children are over-supervised, sometimes instead
they are under-supervised. Maybe they can have their friends over to
drink and smoke pot. Or, since no one can be bothered with them for
long, when they are punished, it is not consistent, or consistently en-
forced. When children get away with something one time but not the
next, only to get away with it again; or if the consequences they are
made to pay under- or overrate the offence in question and are simply
a matter of the parent's mood of the moment then children come to the
conclusion that life is completely unpredictable, and that there is no
value in necessarily doing one thing as opposed to another.

Further, sometimes parents give a certain punishment that in itself
may or may not be reasonable. But in either case, the parent later realizes that enforcement of the punishment will take effort on their part.
So, for example, a week of no TV ends up being only one day—or just
a few hours—without TV. If you lack the patience as a parent not only
to tolerate imperfection but also to tolerate your own rules, then perhaps rethink the rules and/or the punishments. Otherwise, children
again are given mixed signals and feel confused about what in life
they must or mustn't do. And remember that whether it's two hours
or two weeks without TV, the child needs to know you still love him.

Gratitude cannot be forced. In a loving family, as the children get
older their gratitude to those who raised them will naturally unfold.
As adults, they may not think their parents were perfect, but they will
also realize that nobody is. Even if there are minor squabbles from time
to time, for the most part the children respect and appreciate all their
parents have done, and will express this verbally or through gestures
of love.

A loveless family is much more likely to have a 10-, 20-, or 50-year-
old member who would *like* to feel grateful because she knows she
is supposed to, but truly cannot. With few, if any, good memories to
look back on, it is next to impossible to have much appreciation for the
people who technically brought you into the world. Yes, they managed

not to literally murder you, but had few positive effects in your life. The bad seems to relentlessly outweigh the good. And true forgiveness— not just mouthing the words, "I forgive you"—can take years of hard work. Out of a fear of abandonment or coming across as not a nice person, an unloved child may thank the people who raised her. But that doesn't mean she really means it. Moreover, in loveless families, the gesture usually is not returned. The parental figure does not say back, "Well, and thank you for being you and enriching my life."

In fact, it is when love is in peril—or already gone—when people fall back on, "You should be grateful to me after all I've done for you." The same is true in reverse—if essentially the child was the real parent, the parent is unlikely to express sincere gratitude to the child when there is no love.

Afterword: Forgiveness

It is often said that forgiving another person is as much for you as it is for them. We often are told that the only way we ourselves can let go of someone whom we feel has seriously wronged us is to forgive them. But in my experience anyway, forgiveness has proven more complicated than this.

As an adult, I certainly understand how difficult life can be, that no one is perfect, most people did the best they can, you can't take back the past, today is today, don't cut off your nose to spite your face, and so on. I myself have no children, and have found that even raising a strong-willed dog took more patience than I knew I had. When my dog chewed up something I treasured the same day I had the flu, but I still had to walk and feed the dog, I got a little taste of what parents go through for 18 years. Most important of all, when I look back on my life, I can see that there were many, *many* times in which I treated people badly—I was insensitive or outright mean. In short, life has frequently taught me lessons in humility, and I would like to believe that at least some of the time I have absorbed these lessons. Insofar as my family is concerned, a certain peace was made over the years with numerous people, and I suppose we became slightly closer. However, at the same time, I am as of this moment estranged from other family members. There is something of a seesaw effect in my family. If you like people from Group A you can't like people in Group B, and vice versa.

Yet even with all I know in theory, my brain and my heart do not always agree. I do *not* spend 24/7 obsessing on the past. If nothing else, I am much too busy. However, I have an exceptionally good long-term memory, which sometimes seems more like a curse than a blessing. So I can recall entire episodes of life from when I was quite young—who said what to whom where. And from time to time—for some reason especially in the early evening—I find myself getting angry all over again over something that happened many years ago. The person it involved may no longer be living, or perhaps even apologized in some way, and technically I accepted the gesture. But somewhere inside me are wounds that to this day have not completely healed. Some have, but some haven't. I continue to work on these issues in my own way. But I wanted to say all this just in case you, like me, find forgiveness to have a fleeting effect that comes and goes.

I have come to the conclusion that part of my problem has been that *true* forgiveness takes hard work—not to mention courage. All too often, I instead have engaged in what I'll call *wimpy forgiveness.* By this I mean that I've had golden opportunities to sit down truly and make things right, but I wimped out. Following are some simplified examples of wimpy forgiveness that I have been guilty of.

Record-speed forgiveness: Someone might say to me, "I'm sorry I tormented you for 10 years," and I'll reply, "Oh, that's okay," and change the subject. The unexpectedness of the apology catches me off guard, and in the moment I am so pleased to hear this that I want to grab it while I can. I am afraid that belaboring the issue will make the apology go away. I feel good for maybe the rest of that day, but then over time I feel like I cheated myself—and I did. I do not feel that I am now on an even keel with this person; I feel that he still has the upper hand. I had a chance to unburden years or even decades of resentment by sharing how I felt, and instead I decided to keep it all inside. I was too afraid of risking more rejection.

Un-forgiveness forgiveness: Someone hurls hurtful remarks at me. Then when I see her or she emails me it is as though nothing happened. The other person may or may not make a point of smiling, or saying something nice. From this, I am supposed to glean that the nastiness is over. And though the person will not come right out and say it, I am supposed to infer that he is sorry. Since it's such a relief not to be called names anymore, I play right along with it.

While there is much to be said for moving on and letting sleeping dogs lie, when the issue is quite a big deal it may be advisable to wake the dog up, at least for a few minutes. This may mean—gulp!—having to bring up what happened yourself, which is not always an easy thing to do. You don't have to spend hours on it, but in a calm way you can pull the person aside and say that your feelings were hurt, and that you don't want to go through this with the person again. (And if she does do it again, and you do not have to keep associating with her, feel free to let her go.) Otherwise, I have found that over time this un-forgiveness forgiveness simply enables the other person to turn nasty again whenever she or he feels like it. And my own hurt and anger only temporarily goes away.

Fear-behind-a-smile forgiveness: Some of the people who made my childhood unhappy are no longer living, or else quite a lot older. Yet even though I am a grown up myself now and they have no more control over me, I am still, on some level, afraid of them. Yes, even the dead ones. And even if the living ones are nicer to me now. This holds true of people I encounter in the present as well. I know intellectu-ally that they cannot really do anything to me, and certainly by now I have had years of experience with getting yelled at or insulted. In all honesty, I've done my fair share of it right back. When I was younger I usually was too afraid to defend myself, but not anymore. Though at one time it would've been impossible for me, there have even been times I have *started* the argument. So there!

Still, even when I stand up for myself, even when I technically have won the argument, I cannot quite accept that this is what happened, because I am so used to losing. When I act all smiley and nice around someone I am (still) afraid of, afterwards I usually feel that something ugly just happened. And it did. I was dishonest, and I was not kind to myself.

I'll-take-the-blame forgiveness: Someone says to me, "I'm sorry I lied to you," and I'll reply with something like, "Well, I could've figured out the truth if I really wanted to, so there's no reason for you to feel bad." To some extent this is true. As the old saying goes, it takes two to tangle—or tango, as the expression sometimes is phrased. But to use another well-worn saying, I throw out the baby with the bathwater. I not only apologize for my share of the misunderstanding, but shoulder the burden of the other person's mistakes. So I give myself the worst of both worlds. Small wonder if I cannot let go of what happened over time.

As an adult, if I argue with someone I often end up apologizing not just for arguing, but even for the issues I was arguing for or against. I have had to learn to say: "While I stand by what I said the other day, I could've said it better, and I'm sorry if it upset you."

Forgiveness in a vacuum: If someone is no longer living, next to im-possible to get hold of, or I just don't want to face him, I sometimes try to rationalize my bad feelings away by reminding myself of any number of things: "She had a bad childhood, too," "He isn't very smart—not everyone is," "It was XYZ many years ago," "I've done the same thing to other people," or "I learned things from the experience"—hopefully you get the idea. But thoughts and moods are changeable, so these grand conclusions have a way of not lasting.

Also, for most people it is difficult for something to feel real when it is all locked up inside your head. Sharing with others—be it family member, friend, professional, or deity—makes our lives seem more consistent and normalized.

As I just mentioned, true forgiveness takes work and courage. You have to be willing to take your own self seriously—silly as it may sound, you have to protect yourself with your life, and know that you are worth it. Believe it not, it was a major step for me when someone said, "I apologize," and I replied, "I accept your apology," rather than, "Oh, that's okay." There have even been instances in which I have not immediately afterwards said, "I apologize, too," when there was nothing for me to apologize for. (If there *was* something for me to apologize for, that's a different story.) But I was not taught that I mattered, so I was not taught how to protect myself, or that I was even worth protecting. Anything along these lines that I *have* learned, I've had to learn on my own.

When people kill, rape, molest, or physically injure, an entire other process may be called for, and it could be that no real forgiveness is possible—or even the point. Yet at one point in my life, if someone had tried to murder me, I wonder if I would've just said, "Oh, that's okay." That's how little I thought I mattered. Learning otherwise has required courage. Not the same kind of courage it takes to accomplish physical challenges, but a kind of courage nonetheless. Because when you don't like yourself, you may well be afraid of what you'll find when you look inside—as if averting your eyes from a scary movie.

Forgiveness also requires a willingness to communicate. It doesn't have to take years or even days—a single sentence has resolved several long-standing conflicts for me. But it's the difference between having the courage to speak up for yourself, or not—to still believe that others have rightful power over you, or not. To believe that you are worth defending.

Now, having said this, it could very well be that some of the living demons of your past have extremely serious problems. If they are alcoholics, or substance abusers, or have a mental disorder, you may not make much progress with them, and you may, in fact, put yourself in a vulnerable position if you push them too far. When someone literally is on her deathbed—coping with mortality, pain, and side effects from medication—it may be inappropriate of you to pick that moment to say something like, "40 years ago, why did you borrow my shirt without asking?" Some things really do need to be put to rest. If a relatively trivial matter bothers you for a long time, there reaches a point in which it's your problem, not anyone else's. But if someone hasn't long to go or his mind is deteriorating, and he says something like, "Please know I always loved you," that may well be as good as it's going to get.

In other words, using common sense is also part of respecting and taking good care of yourself. You don't want to do something you'll regret. But if the individual in question is reasonably approachable, and that little voice inside you is urging you to speak up, try it and see what happens. *Care* enough to try. It's not a matter of accusing or blaming. It's a matter of saying, "I was a human being, I had feelings, and it really hurt me when you used to make fun of me," or whatever it was that happened. If you're angry that no one knows the real you... then give them something of the real you. Your past gave you a thousand good reasons not to trust this person—or maybe not to trust anybody—but on the other hand, as time moves on some people do change for the better.

In a loveless family, it is all too easy to fall back on the wimpy and mediocre, "Oh, that's okay," rather than seeing an opportunity for honesty—which can lead to actual closeness. It is a vicious cycle: no one cares about anyone else, so even when someone tries to apologize there's no reason to take it seriously. Because taking it seriously would mean that you cared, and you'd just as soon get a root canal than let these jerks think they matter to you. There is a passive–aggressive hostility behind, "Oh, that's okay." In a way, it is saying: "I am superior to you, and what you say or do is of little consequence to me." It also may signal intense cynicism. You don't believe anything can change, so you'll just say something brief and polite rather than deal with it. Sometimes it is a razor-thin line between feeling inferior and feeling superior. So the two people involved go from being estranged to being estranged. Nothing of lasting value was communicated. Oddly enough, 5 or 10 years later, the same old business comes up yet again, because it was never really resolved in the first place.

If you and the other party have said all you need to say, you probably still need some time within yourself to process it all. Before sending the person an effusive message out of fear of abandonment, wait at least a few days if possible, and then see how you feel. Share what happened with people you trust, including a therapist if you have one. If you are spiritual, pray or meditate about it. If you are artistic, write or draw something about it. If you are athletic, run some laps around the football field about it. If you like to be in nature, go on a camping trip about it. Hopefully you get the idea. But take it seriously, because you owe it to yourself to take your own self seriously.

And then, maybe, you may find that you like or even love this person you thought you hated.

Let there be love.

Notes

Introduction

1. Staff Writer, "Statistics on Domestic Violence in the United States," http://www.soundvision.com/Info/domesticviolence/statistics.asp.

2. "National Statistics," Domestic Violence Resource Center, http://www.dvrcor.org/domestic/violence/resources/C61/.

3. Ibid.

4. Vincent Iannelli, "Child Abuse Statistics: Child Abuse Basics," http://pediatrics.about.com/od/childabuse/a/05_abuse_stats.htm.

5. "National Child Abuse Statistics: Child Abuse in America," Childhelp, http://www.childhelp.org/pages/statistics.

6. Ibid.

7. "UNODC Homicide Statistics," United Nations Office on Drugs and Crime, http://www.unodc.org/unodc/en/data-and-analysis/homicide.html; Roy Walmsley, "World Prison Population List," International Centre for Prison Studies, King's College, London, http://www.answerbag.com/q_view/1868620.

Chapter 1: What Is a Loveless Family?

1. Jia A. Son, National Resource Center for Foster Care and Permanency Planning at the Hunter College School of Social Work, *Information Packet: Runaway and Homeless Youth* (2002).

2. Peter J. Burke, "Identity Control Theory," in *Blackwell Encyclopedia of Sociology*, vol. 5, ed. George Ritzer (Malden, MA: Blackwell, 2007), 2202–7.

3. Susie Scott, "The Shell, the Stranger, and the Competent Other: Towards a Sociology of Shyness," *Sociology* 38 (2004): 121–37.

4. Ibid.

5. George H. Mead, *Mind, Self, and Society* (Chicago: University of Chicago Press, 1934).

6. Claire N. Kowalski, "Smother Love vs. Tough Love," *Social Work* 21, no. 4 (1977): 319–21.

7. Elijah Mickel and Cecilia Hall, "Choosing to Love: The Essentials of Loving (Presents and Problems)," *International Journal of Reality Therapy* 27, no. 2 (2008): 30–34.

8. Dan P. McAdams et al., "Family Metaphors and Moral Institutions: How Conservatives and Liberals Narrate Their Lives," *Journal of Personality & Social Psychology* 95, no. 4 (2008): 978–90.

9. Amir Abbassi and Aslinia S. Dean, "Family Violence, Trauma and Social Learning Theory," *Journal of Professional Counseling: Practice, Theory & Research* 38, no. 1 (2010): 16–27.

Chapter 2: What a Loveless Family Does to You

1. Here, you may find that you are still unable to truly let go of your past and be happy in the present moment.

2. The way you feel about yourself inside does not, therefore, actually match with your exterior success.

3. You will tend to be more familiar with feelings of unhappiness, linked to feeling insecure, and to not having the belief that things can go well for you.

4. You may find that you cannot keep the good deeds or acts of others in their true perspective when they are aimed at you.

5. The lack of love in your formative years leads toward an inconsistent identity and interactions with others.

Chapter 3: The Star Syndrome

1. John Maltby, "An Interest in Fame: Confirming the Measurement and Empirical Conceptualization of Fame Interest," *British Journal of Psychology* 101, no. 3 (2010): 411–32.

2. Joshua D. Miller, Thomas A. Widiger, and W. Keith Campbell, "Narcissistic Personality Disorder and the DSM-V," *Journal of Abnormal Psychology* 119, no. 4 (2010): 640–49.

3. Daniel Shaw, "Enter Ghosts: The Loss of Intersubjectivity in Clinical Work with Adult Children of Pathological Narcissists," *Psychoanalytic Dialogues* 20, no. 1 (2010): 46–59.

Chapter 4: The Bad Example Syndrome

1. Richard J. Loewenstein, "Dissociation of the 'Bad' Parent, Preservation of the 'Good' Parent," *Psychiatry: Interpersonal & Biological Processes* 67, no. 3 (2004): 256–60.

2. Deborah H. Gruenfeld et al., "Power and the Objectification of Social Targets," *Journal of Personality & Social Psychology* 95, no. 1 (2008): 111–27.

3. Daniel Shaw, "Enter Ghosts: The Loss of Intersubjectivity in Clinical Work with Adult Children of Pathological Narcissists," *Psychoanalytic Dialogues* 20, no. 1 (2010): 46–59.

4. W. Lauder et al., "Developing Self-Neglect Theory: Analysis of Related and Atypical Cases of People Identified as Self-Neglecting," *Journal of Psychiatric & Mental Health Nursing* 16, no. 5 (1999): 447–54.

5. Elaine F. Jones et al., "Character Disposition and Behavior Type: Influences of Valence on Preschool Children's Social Judgments," *Journal of Genetic Psychology* 170, no. 4 (2009): 310–25.

6. Alan Woolfolk, "The Denial of Character," *Society* 39, no. 3 (2002): 25–33.

7. Kirby Deater-Deckard et al., "Sibling Relationships and Social-Emotional Adjustment in Different Family Contexts," *Social Development* 11 (2002): 571–90.

Chapter 5: The Frenemy Syndrome

1. Christopher J. Hopwood et al., "The Construct Validity of Passive-Aggressive Personality Disorder," *Psychiatry: Interpersonal & Biological Processes* 72, no. 3 (2009): 256–67.

2. If you were bullied when you were young then you are often afraid to speak up.

3. Jeffrey G. Johnson et al., "Cumulative Prevalence of Personality Disorders between Adolescence and Adulthood," *Acta Psychiatrica Scandinavica* 118, no. 5 (2008): 410–13.

4. Usha Kumar et al., "Identity Status and Preference of Managerial Styles," *Journal of Social Psychology* 110, no. 2 (1980): 295.

5. Elizabeth Lynch, "Lasting Damage," *Nursing Standard* 18, no. 45 (2004): 22–23.

Chapter 6: The Ostrich Syndrome

1. Russell R. Dynes, Alfred C. Clarke, and Simon Dinitz, "Levels of Occupational Aspiration: Some Aspects of Family Experience as a Variable," *American Sociological Review* 21, no. 2 (1956): 212–21.

2. Ibid.

3. Ibid.

4. Nadia Sorkhabi, "Sources of Parent-Adolescent Conflict: Content and Form of Parenting," *Social Behavior & Personality: An International Journal* 38, no. 6 (2010): 761–82.

Chapter 7: The Clueless Meddler Syndrome

1. Richard C. Page and Daniel N. Berkow, "Concepts of the Self: Western and Eastern Perspectives," *Journal of Multicultural Counseling & Development* 19, no. 2 (1991): 83–93.

2. Deborah Finfgeld-Connett, "Clarification of Social Support," *Journal of Nursing Scholarship* 37, no. 1 (2005): 4–9.

3. Anthea Symonds, "Angels and Interfering Busybodies: The Social Construction of Two Occupations," *Sociology of Health & Illness* 13, no. 2 (1991): 249–64.

Chapter 8: The One-Way Streeter Syndrome

1. Günter H. Seidler, "Shame and Guilt: Self-Reflexive Affects from the Perspective of Relationship and Reciprocity," *American Journal of Psychotherapy* 61, no. 1 (2007): 37–49,

2. Nevelyn N. Trumpeter et al., "Self-Functioning and Perceived Parenting: Relations of Parental Empathy and Love Inconsistency with Narcissism, Depression, and Self-Esteem," *Journal of Genetic Psychology* 169, no. 1 (2008): 51–71.

3. Ibid.

4. Judy Parkinson and Patrick Parkinson, "Children's Participation in Family Law Disputes: The Views of Children, Parents, Lawyers and Counsellors," *Family Matters* 82 (2009): 15–21.

5. Paul Gilbert et al., "Self-Criticism and Self-Warmth: An Imagery Study Exploring Their Relation to Depression," *Journal of Cognitive Psychotherapy* 20, no. 2 (2006): 183–200.

Chapter 9: The Short-Distance Runner Syndrome

1. Katie M. Lindblom and Matt J. Gray, "Relationship Closeness and Trauma Narrative Detail: A Critical Analysis of Betrayal Trauma Theory," *Applied Cognitive Psychology* 24, no. 1 (2010): 1–19.

2. Paulette Rozencwajg and Denis Corroyer, "Cognitive Processes in the Reflective–Impulsive Cognitive Style," *Journal of Genetic Psychology* 166, no. 4 (2005): 451–63.

3. Nedim Karakayali, "Social Distance and Affective Orientations," *Sociological Forum* 24, no. 3 (2009): 538–62.

4. Nola L. Passmore and Judith A. Feeney, "Reunions of Adoptees Who Have Met Both Birth Parents: Post-Reunion Relationships and Factors That Facilitate and Hinder the Reunion Process," *Adoption Quarterly*12, no. 2 (2009): 100–119.

5. Stacey R. Bloomer, Theresa Ann Sipe, and Danielle E. Ruedt, "Support Payment and Child Visitation: Perspectives from Nonresident Fathers and Resident Mothers," *Journal of Sociology & Social Welfare* 29, no. 2 (2002): 77–92.

Chapter 10: The Volcano Syndrome

1. Georganna Sedlar and David J. Hansen, "Anger, Child Behavior, and Family Distress: Further Evaluation of the Parental Anger Inventory," *Journal of Family Violence* 16, no. 4 (2001): 361–73.

2. Joachim Stöber, "Self–Pity: Exploring the Links to Personality, Control Beliefs, and Anger," *Journal of Personality* 71, no. 2 (2003): 183–220.

3. Cynthia Arnold, "An Ocean of Emotion: Mood Swings, Anger, and Uncontrollable Laughing and Crying," *Inside MS* 18, no. 2 (2000): 59–62.

4. Barbro Wijma et al., "Cycles of Abuse Nurtured by Concealment: A Clinical Report," *Journal of Psychosomatic Obstetrics & Gynecology* 28, no. 3 (2007): 155–60.

5. Justin W. Patchin and Sameer Hinduja, "Cyberbullying and Self-Esteem," *Journal of School Health* 80, no. 12 (2010): 614–21.

6. Murray Meisels and Michael A. Dosey, "Personal Space, Anger-Arousal, and Psychological Defense," *Journal of Personality* 39, no. 3 (1971): 333–44; Roy F. Baumeister, Arlene Stillwell, and Sara R. Wotman, "Victim and Perpetrator Accounts of Interpersonal Conflict: Autobiographical Narratives about Anger," *Journal of Personality & Social Psychology* 59, no. 5 (1990): 994–1005.

Chapter 11: The Iron Butterfly Syndrome

1. Marylene Cloitre et al., "Attachment Organization, Emotion Regulation, and Expectations of Support in a Clinical Sample of Women with Childhood Abuse Histories," *Journal of Traumatic Stress* 21, no. 3 (2008): 282–89.

2. John B. Nezlek, Astrid Schütz, and Ina Sellin, "Self-Presentational Success in Daily Social Interaction," *Self & Identity* 6, no. 4 (2007): 361–79.

3. Elke Zeijl et al., "The Role of Parents and Peers in the Leisure Activities of Young Adolescents," *Journal of Leisure Research* 32, no. 3 (2000): 281–303.

4. D. S. Neil Van Leeuwen, "Self-Deception Won't Make You Happy," *Social Theory & Practice* 35, no. 1 (2009): 107–32.

Chapter 12: The Interloper Syndrome

1. Tamara D. Afifi and Loreen Olson, "The Chilling Effect in Families and the Pressure to Conceal Secrets," *Communication Monographs* 72, no. 2 (2005): 192–216.

2. Ibid.

3. Stewart R. Clegg and Ad van Itersdon, "Dishing the Dirt: Gossiping in Organizations," *Culture & Organization* 15, nos. 3/4 (2009): 275–89.

4. Margaret M. Mahoney, "Stepparents as Third Parties in Relation to Their Stepchildren," *Family Law Quarterly* 40, no. 1 (2006): 81–108.

5. Jina H. Yoo, "The Power of Sharing Negative Information in a Dyadic Context," *Communication Reports* 22, no. 1 (2009): 29–40.

Chapter 13: Dealing with Serious Physical Conditions

1. Hanoch Livneh, Sheri M. Lott, and Richard F. Antonak, "Patterns of Psychosocial Adaptation to Chronic Illness and Disability: A Cluster Analytic Approach," *Psychology, Health & Medicine* 9, no. 4 (2004): 411–30.

2. Holly E. Recchia and Nina Howe, "Sibling Relationship Quality Moderates the Associations between Parental Interventions and Siblings' Independent Conflict Strategies and Outcomes," *Journal of Family Psychology* 23, no. 4 (2009): 551–61.

3. Lauren J. Breen, "Early Childhood Service Delivery for Families Living with Childhood Disability: Disabling Families Through Problematic Implicit Ideology," *Australasian Journal of Early Childhood* 34, no. 4 (2009): 14–21.

Chapter 14: Dealing with Serious Mental Conditions

1. Michael Buxton, "Interpreting Children's Mental Health Problems," *Mental Health Practice* 14, no. 3 (2010): 16–20.

2. Matteo Selvini, "Severe Mental Disorders and Distorted Reality," *American Journal of Family Therapy* 24, no. 2 (1996): 107–16; Patrick Corrigan and Frederick Miller, "Shame, Blame, and Contamination: A Review of the Impact of Mental Illness Stigma on Family Members," *Journal of Mental Health* 13, no. 6 (2004): 537–48.

3. Joanne L. Riebschleger, "Families of Chronically Mentally Ill People: Siblings Speak to Social Workers," *Health & Social Work* 16, no. 2 (1991): 94–103.

4. Ibid.

Chapter 15: Dealing with Death

1. Joseph A. Amato, "Death, and the Stories We Don't Have," *Monist* 76, no. 2 (1993): 252–70.

2. Dorothy P. Rice and Norman Fineman, "Economic Implications of Increased Longevity in the United States," *Annual Review of Public Health* 25, no. 1 (2004): 457–73.

3. Yang Sungeun and Paul C. Rosenblatt, "Couple Rage and Emotional Distancing When a Partner is Dying," *Journal of Loss & Trauma* 12, no. 4 (2007): 305–20.

4. Barry Richards, "The Anatomy of Envy," *Psychoanalytic Studies* 2, no. 1 (2000): 65–76.

Chapter 16: Finding Lasting Friendship

1. Karen L. Fingerman, Elizabeth L. Hay, and Kira S. Birditt, "The Best of Ties, the Worst of Ties: Close, Problematic, and Ambivalent Social Relationships," *Journal of Marriage & Family* 66, no. 3 (2004): 792–808.

2. Ibid.

3. Clare M. Stocker and Melissa K. Richmond, "Longitudinal Associations between Hostility in Adolescents' Family Relationships and Friendships and Hostility in Their Romantic Relationships," *Journal of Family Psychology* 21, no. 3 (2007): 490–97.

4. Gita Venkataramani Johar, "The Price of Friendship: When, Why, and How Relational Norms Guide Social Exchange Behavior," *Journal of Consumer Psychology (Lawrence Erlbaum Associates)* 15, no. 1 (2005): 22–27.

Chapter 17: Finding Lasting Intimacy

1. Peter J. Stein, "Singlehood: An Alternative to Marriage," *Family Coordinator* 24, no. 4 (1975): 489–504.

2. Shlomo Hareli and Ursula Hess, "What Emotional Reactions Can Tell Us about the Nature of Others: An Appraisal Perspective on Person Perception," *Cognition & Emotion* 24, no. 1 (2010): 128–40.

3. Dustin Wood, Peter Harms, and Simine Vazire, "Perceiver Effects as Projective Tests: What Your Perceptions of Others Say about You," *Journal of Personality & Social Psychology* 99, no. 1 (2010): 174–90.

4. Andrew J. Cherlin, "The Origins of the Ambivalent Acceptance of Divorce," *Journal of Marriage & Family* 71, no. 2 (2009): 226–29.

Chapter 18: Relating to Children

1. Helga Sneddon, Dorota Iwaniec, and Moira C. Stewart, "Prevalence of Childhood Abuse in Mothers Taking Part in a Study of Parenting Their Own Children," *Child Abuse Review* 19, no. 1 (2010): 39–55.

2. Ibid.

3. Michael Ungar, "Overprotective Parenting: Helping Parents Provide Children the Right Amount of Risk and Responsibility," *American Journal of Family Therapy* 37, no. 3 (2009): 258–71.

4. Geoffrey L. Brown et al., "Young Children's Self-Concepts: Associations with Child Temperament, Mothers' and Fathers' Parenting, and Triadic Family Interaction," *Merrill-Palmer Quarterly* 55, no. 2 (2009): 184–216.

5. Karol L. Kumpfer, "Why Are There no Effective Child Abuse Prevention Parenting Interventions?" *Substance Use & Misuse* 43, nos. 8/9 (2008): 1262–65.

Index

About the Author

JON P. BLOCH, a former runaway who was periodically homeless as a youth, is chair of the Sociology Department at Southern Connecticut State University. In addition to his scholarly research in areas such as social theory, religion, and gender, Dr. Bloch is the author of such books as *The Everything Health Guide to Adult Bipolar Disorder* and *The Bipolar Relationship*. He has also published numerous works of fiction.